Paleo Cook

2 Boc

100 Slow Cooker and Baking Recipes

By

Patrick Smith

ISBN-10: 1511483008
ISBN-13: 978-1511483001

Contents

Introduction: The Paleo Diet

"Paleo" refers to the "Paleolithic era", otherwise known as the "Stone Age", in which mankind lived in the wild, ate natural foods that were available and weren't grown or otherwise produced.

We know that peoples and tribes that still live in this manner are unusually healthy. For example, the Tokelauan people and their neighbors, who live on islands in the South Pacific, get most of their daily calories from coconuts.

Coconuts are extremely rich in "good" saturated fatty acids. In consequence, the Tokelauans consume more saturated fats than anyone else in the world – even more than an obese American. However, they are built like Olympic athletes. Heart disease, diabetes, depression and other modern diseases of civilization are unheard of among them.

The secret of their health is the natural foods they eat. We also know this to be true for Eskimos, even though they eat whale, which is very rich in fat as well.

Aligning with these results, the paleo diet wants you to eat natural foods, such as fish, organic meat produced from free ranging cows, coconut products and so on. On the other hand, it doesn't want you to eat beans, peas, dairy products or grains, which means no noodles, no bread and a lot of other foods.

The real problems to our health are processed foods, the chemicals and so called trans fats that are being used or created in these processes. We know today that trans fats are what cause heart disease, because they clog arteries. In fact, at the end of 2013, the US Food and Drug Administration decided to ban trans fats, so they are going to be weeded out of the foods in America, an enormous victory for medical science that has been fighting for this for decades. It is likely the rest of the world will follow this example in time.

To be paleo, all foods must be organic. This is especially critical when it comes to meat.

Ordinary meat comes from cattle raised on corn instead of grass. To produce this meat, the animals are first pumped full of growth hormones to make them insanely hungry, because otherwise they won't eat the corn. They instinctively know their stomach isn't built for this kind of food, but with the hormone-induced hunger, they are driven to eat it. The corn turns their stomach so acidic that it becomes a seething cauldron of bacterial growth. Now the cow has to be pumped full of antibiotics to ensure it won't die of an infection.

That mess is what you consume, if you don't go for organic meat. Why do we do this to our cows, you ask? It makes them grow really fast, so a farmer can sell more meat per month. Organic meat is more expensive, because the farmers that produce it have less to sell and need to raise the price to compensate.

Not all people choose a 100% paleo lifestyle and wish to supplement with some non-paleo ingredients. This choice is perfectly fine, because we have some healthy foods today that simply were not available to people in the Stone Age.

If you choose to live semi-paleo, go for whole-grains, be it rice, noodles or bread. Never go for white noodles, white rice or white bread. These are not whole-grain and have almost no nutritional value. White bread in particular is so empty, it turns into a doe like paste in your stomach. It is only something to fill yourself with so the hunger goes away, but gives your body nothing to work with. You can also go for occasional beans and peas, since they are great sources of iron.

Now, let's start cooking!

Patrick Smith

Book 1: Paleo Slow Cooker Recipes

Section 1: Paleo Food Replacements

Since rice, noodles and potatoes are not paleo, we need to use alternatives.

The standard paleo replacement for rice is **cauliflower rice**. It is made entirely from cauliflower and simulates rice much better than most people think before they try it.

The only type of potato that works with the paleo diet are **sweet potatoes**. Simply use them instead of other potato types.

For noodles, you can either make egg noodles with **almond flour** or **coconut flour** instead if regular flour, or you can slice **Zucchinis** into noodle shapes.

In this section, I explain how to make the rice and Zucchini noodles.

1. Paleo Cauliflower Rice

Cauliflower rice is the standard paleo replacement for regular rice. As the name suggests, it is made entirely from cauliflower.

30 oz. (850 g) **cauliflower** (chopped coarsely)
1 **onion** (chopped finely)
1 ½ tbs **coconut oil**
2 tbs **coconut butter**
Salt and **pepper**

Makes 6 servings
Calories: 40 per serving

Remove leaves and discolored parts from the cauliflower, then chop into chunks. Place in a food processor and hack until the parts are the size of regular rice grains.

Heat the coconut butter and coconut oil in a skillet and sauté the onions until translucent. Add the cauliflower rice and distribute evenly.

Season the mix with salt and pepper or other seasonings of your choice.

Cover and cook for 7-10 minutes.

2. Paleo Zucchini Noodles

There are two ways to replace pasta that I use myself.

One way is to use almond flour or coconut flour instead of regular flour and make grain-free paleo noodles from scratch.

Another way is to turn Zucchinis into spaghetti, which is quick and easy.

6 Zucchinis
Salt and **pepper**

Makes 4 servings
Calories: 38 per serving

There is an easy and a slightly harder way to do this.

The harder way is to use a julienne peeler to cut the Zucchinis into slices.

The easy way is to use a spiral slicer, which you probably have to buy first. You can find them on Amazon.

Fry the noodles in a skillet using coconut oil, or microwave them on a high setting for 2-3 minutes.

Section 2: Main Dishes

1. Barbecue Chicken

This is a tangy and sweet barbeque chicken. It goes well with sweet potatoes or cauliflower rice, which is no grain and suitable for the paleo diet.

24 oz. (680 g) **boneless chicken breast**
¼ cup **Italian dressing**
1 tbs **Worcestershire sauce**
2 tbs **chicken broth**
¾ cup organic **barbeque sauce**
2 tbs **arrowroot flour** or **coconut flour**

Makes 8 servings
Calories: 170 per serving

Place the chicken at the bottom of the slow cooker. Mix the dressing, barbeque sauce and Worcestershire sauce in a container, then stir to combine.

Pour over the chicken and cook for 5 hours on low heat.

Remove the chicken and set aside on a cutting board to cool for a few minutes. Shred the chicken into pieces.

Combine the flour of your choice and chicken broth in a bowl. Slowly add into the sauce and cover until it is thick and heated through.

Return the chicken and continue to cook for another 45 minutes.

Enjoy!

2. Family Chilaquiles

Chilaquiles is a Mexican favorite that combines cilantro, chipotle and chicken. There are many ways to prepare Chilaquiles. This one is less traditional, but a family favorite.

The paleo tortillas used in this recipe are explained in recipe 9a.

4 **chicken breasts**
1 ¼ cups **red bell pepper** (shredded)
¾ cup **chicken broth**
1 tbs **cumin** (ground)
6 **garlic cloves**
4 oz. (110 g) **green chilies** (chopped)
2/3 cup **queso fresco** (crumbled)
1 ½ cup **red onion** (chopped)
1 ¼ cups **green bell pepper** (chopped)
¼ cup fresh **cilantro**
2 tbs **chili** (chopped)
50 oz. (1.4 kg) **tomatoes** (roasted)
5 cups **paleo tortillas** from recipe 9a

Makes 10 servings
Calories: 220 per serving

Follow recipe 9a to make the paleo tortillas.

Heat a large pan over medium heat. Place the chicken at the bottom, then cook for 3 to 4 minutes on each side. Cook until golden brown.

Mix the onion, red bell pepper, green bell pepper, low sodium chicken broth, fresh cilantro, cumin, chipotle, garlic cloves, tomatoes and green chilies. Place the mix in a slow cooker.

Remove the chicken from the pan and transfer it to the cooker. Cover and cook for 4 hours on medium heat.

Remove the chicken from the slow cooker and the meat from the bones. Return the chicken into the soup.

Divide into bowls and ladle the soup over the paleo tortillas.

Enjoy!

3. Mediterranean Chicken Meal

Mediterranean recipes are often dominated by ingredients such as lemon, olives and tomatoes. Serve this dish with mashed sweet potatoes. Remember to use organic meat.

1 **lemon**
¼ cup **olives**
15 oz. (425 g) **plum tomatoes** (roughly chopped)
¼ tsp **black pepper** (ground)
¾ cup **onion** (chopped)
2 tbs **drained capers**
12 bone in **chicken thighs**
1 tbs **olive oil** or **coconut oil**
Rosemary (optional, chopped)
Fresh parsley (optional, chopped)

Makes 6 servings
Calories: 215 per serving

Grate the lemon to get 1 tbs of zest. Also, squeeze the lemon to get 1 tbs of juice. Combine the zest and juice in a bowl. Cover and refrigerate.

Combine the onion, lemon juice, olives, drained capers and plum tomatoes in a slow cooker. Season the chicken thighs with pepper.

Heat the oil of your choice in a pan over medium heat. Place the chicken thighs in a pan, then cook for 3 minutes on each side until brown.

Add the chicken thighs to the slow cooker. Cook for 4 hours on medium heat until brown and tender.

Place the chicken on plates and stir in the lemon sauce.

Garnish with desired amount of rosemary and parsley.

4. Apple Chicken

This recipe is rich in taste. It combines chicken, apples and herbs and produces a delicious smell in your house.

2 lb. (900 g) **chicken breasts** (boneless, skinless)
2 **apples** (cored, sliced)
2 **garlic cloves** (smashed)
1 **bay leaf**
2/3 cups **chicken broth**
1 **onion** (sliced)
2 tbs **ginger** (grated)
1 tsp **cinnamon**
½ tsp **paprika**
1 tsp **salt**
1/2 tsp **pepper**

Makes 15 servings
Calories: 270 per serving

Combine the chicken broth, onions and chicken breasts in a slow cooker.

Add the apples on top and sprinkle with the spices, then top with the bay leaf.

Cover and set to low heat. Cook for 9 hours.

Remove and shred the chicken. This dish goes well with roasted sweet potatoes.

Enjoy!

5. Stuffed Bell Peppers

This is a quick and easy dish that you can prepare in just 15 minutes and leave for 4 hours.

¾ cup **water**
8 oz. (225 g) organic **spicy sausage**
¼ tsp **pepper** (ground)
4 small red bell peppers
½ cup **cauliflower rice** (see section 1)
1/8 tbs **salt**
½ cup **garlic**
½ cup **coconut cream**
2 tbs **basil** (sliced)

Makes 4 servings
Calories: 305 per serving

Bring the water to a boil in a small pan. Stir in cauliflower rice, then remove from heat. Cover and set aside for 5 minutes.

Remove the casing from the sausage and cook in a pan over medium heat for 5 until it is done. Stir to crumble. Remove from heat and set aside.

Add the salt and pepper. Stir in the coconut cream.

Cut the tops of the bell peppers and remove seeds and flesh inside. Sprinkle with salt and scoop the sausage mixture into the peppers. Return the pepper tops.

Place the stuffed peppers in a slow cooker, set to low heat and cook for 4 hours or until tender. Garnish the pepper with basil and coconut cream if desired.

Enjoy!

6. Chicken Thighs with Tomato and Olives

12 **chicken thighs**
¼ tsp **black pepper** (ground)
1 ½ tbs **garlic** (minced)
3 tbs **tomato paste**
28 oz. (800 g) **tomatoes** (diced)
2 tbs **flat leaf parsley** (chopped)
1 tsp **salt**
1 tsp **olive oil**
3 tbs **crushed red pepper**
¼ cup **olives** (pitted)

Makes 6 servings
Calories: 250 per serving

Season the chicken with salt and pepper. Heat the oil in a pan and sauté the chicken for 2 minutes on each side until browned.

Place the chicken inside the slow cooker and add garlic, then stir occasionally. Scrape the bottom of the pan to remove browned bits. Continue to sauté for 30 seconds.

Add the red pepper, tomato paste and tomatoes. Cover, set heat to high and cook for 4 hours.

If desired, add more parsley, olives and seasoning for more flavors. Add the parsley last.

Enjoy!

7. Chicken Drummettes with Dip

Chicken drummettes are a classic favorite and can be served with vegetables, cauliflower rice or mashed sweet potato. This recipe contains the option to include some vinegar, which is a "gray ingredient" in the paleo diet and has been adopted by many that follow a paleo lifestyle.

48 oz. (1.36 kg) **chicken wing drums** (skinned)
¾ cup paleo **hot sauce**
1 tsp low-salt **Worcestershire sauce**
Coconut cream (as dip)
28 **carrots**
¼ tsp **black pepper** (ground)
2 tbs **balsamic vinegar** (optional)
2 **garlic cloves** (minced)
28 **celery sticks**

Makes 14 servings
Calories: 100 per serving

Preheat the oven to 450F (230°C). Place foil at the bottom of a jelly roll pan. Coat the foil with cooking spray. Put the chicken in the pan and sprinkle with pepper. Coat the chicken with cooking spray, then bake for 7 minutes until brown.

Combine the hot sauce, optional vinegar, Worcestershire sauce and garlic cloves in a slow cooker.

Remove the chicken from the pot, then drain the excess oil. Put the chicken in the slow cooker and coat with sauce. Cover and cook for 3 hours on high heat or until the chicken is tender.

Serve with carrots sticks, celery sticks and coconut cream as dip.

Enjoy!

8. Spicy Mushrooms

If this recipe included black beans instead of mushrooms and cauliflower rice, it could be a Mexican dish. In case you are wondering, the pumpkin seeds are indeed a paleo ingredient.

8 oz. (225 g) **mushrooms**
8 oz. (225 g) **cauliflower rice**
2 cups **onion** (chopped)
1 tsp **salt**
1 tbs **lime juice**
½ cup fresh **cilantro** (chopped)
3 cups (700 ml) **chicken broth**
1 tbs **chipotle chili** (chopped)
4 **garlic cloves** (minced)
4 oz. (110 g) **coconut cream** (optional)
½ cup **pumpkin seeds** (not salted)

Makes 14 servings
Calories: 160 per serving

Place the mushrooms and cauliflower rice in a Dutch oven and pour water until it covers the ingredients for about 2 inches (5 cm). Cook for 2 minutes on high heat. Remove and allow to cool for an hour, then drain.

Place the mixture in a slow cooker. Stir in the broth, chopped onion, chipotle, salt, and garlic cloves. Cover and cook for 8 hours in low heat.

Add the lime juice and mash the mixture until it is soft and thick. Top with the pumpkin seeds, cilantro and optional coconut cream.

Enjoy!

9a. Paleo Tortillas

Some of the recipes in this book require tortillas. This means you either need to buy paleo tortillas somewhere or make them yourself. Here's how to do it.

4 **eggs**
2 tsp **coconut oil** (melted)
½ cup **arrowroot powder**
2 tsp **coconut flour**
2 pinches of **salt**
½ tsp **vanilla extract** (optional)

Makes six 8 inch (20 cm) tortillas
Calories: 65 per tortilla

Crack the eggs and pour into a bowl. Add the melted coconut oil and whisk.

Add coconut flour, arrowroot powder and salt. Beat well to combine.

Put a skillet over medium heat. Add 1/6 of the tortilla batter and quickly coat the bottom evenly.

Cook for 1 minute on each side. Repeat until six tortillas are made.

After the tortillas are done, they can be stored in an airtight plastic bag or glass container. Let them cool first.

Enjoy!

9b. Stacked Chicken Enchilada

This recipe uses the paleo tortillas from recipe 9a. As always, choose organic meat.

1 tsp **olive oil** or **coconut oil**
½ cup **poblano chili** (chopped)
1 ½ tsp **chipotle chili powder**
8 oz. (225 g) **tomato sauce with garlic, oregano and basil**
2 cups **chicken breast** (shredded)
15 oz. (425 g) **mushrooms**
1 cup **onion** (chopped)
2 **garlic cloves** (minced)
14 oz. (400 g) **tomatoes** (unsalted, diced)
Cooking spray
1 cup **cauliflower rice**
5 **paleo tortillas** from recipe 9a

Makes 9 servings
Calories: 290 per serving

Heat a large pan in medium heat. Add oil in a pan then swirl to coat. Add the chili, garlic and onion in the pan, then sauté for 6 minutes until the vegetables are tender. Stir in the tomato sauce, tomatoes and chili powder.

Place the tomato mixture in a blender and allow steam to escape by removing the center lid. Place a towel at the opening to prevent spills. Blend until smooth. Pour the mixture in a large bowl. Repeat procedure until the tomato mixture is well blended.

Coat the cooker with cooking spray. Place 3 tbs of tomato mixture in a bowl, then add the cauliflower rice, chicken and mushrooms. Place a paleo tortilla in the slow cooker, then pour the chicken mixture. Top with another tortilla. Continue to layer the chicken and tomato mixture in this way. Cook for 2 hours on low heat. Cut into pieces and serve.

10. Satsuma Turkey

The oranges and marmalade provides a sweet and tangy flavor, while the pepper adds a spicy kick to the dish. As always, choose organic meat.

3 cups **red onions** (thinly sliced)
2/3 cup fresh **orange juice**
2 tsp **tamarind paste**
60 oz. (1.7 kg) bone-in **turkey thighs** (skinned)
1 tsp **salt**
2 cups fresh **mandarin orange** (sectioned)
1/3 cup **orange marmalade**
½ tsp **red pepper** (crushed)
2 tsp **five spice powder**
1 tbs **olive oil** or **coconut oil**
1 ½ tbs **arrowroot flour** or **coconut flour**

Makes 8 servings
Calories: 280 per serving

Combine the red onions, orange juice, marmalade, tamarind paste and red pepper in a slow cooker.

Rinse the turkey thighs and dry. Sprinkle with spices. Heat the oil of your choice in a pan over medium heat. Add the turkey thighs to the pan and cook for 3 minutes on each side until browned.

Place the turkey thighs in a single layer over the onion mixture. Add the orange sections and cover. Cook for 4 hours in low heat.

Remove the turkey thighs from the slow cooker, then remove the bones and discard. Transfer to a plate.

To make a sauce, pour ¾ of the cooking liquid and orange sections into a pan.

Combine the flour of your choice and the remaining ¼ of the cooking liquid in a bowl. Whisk until smooth. Add flour mixture to the pan.

Bring the sauce to a boil and cook for 1 minute, stirring continuously until it thickens.

Pour sauce over turkey and serve.

Enjoy!

11. Poblano Pudding

Poblano pudding is a delicious Mexican theme buffet that is a good addition to any meal.

4 **poblano chilies** (chopped)
½ cup **coconut milk**
4 tbs **arrowroot flour** or **coconut flour**
2 tbs **coconut butter**
¼ tsp **salt**
3 cups **cauliflower rice**
1 tbs **coconut cream**
Cooking spray
2 **eggs**

Makes 8 servings
Calories: 175 per serving

Preheat the broiler and place the chilies on a baking sheet. Broil until darkened and charred, typically less than 10 minutes.

Place in a paper bag and close to seal. Set aside for 15 minutes.

Combine the coconut milk, the flour of your choice, coconut butter, salt and eggs in a slow cooker. Stir using a whisk until blended properly.

Add the cauliflower rice, coconut cream and chilies. Cover and cook on low heat for 2 ½ -3 hours.

Remove the lid and cook for another 15 minutes.

Enjoy!

12. Paleo Tortillas with Jicama Slaw

This dish has an exotic and spicy flavor, combining seasoning and spices. It contains the option to include some vinegar, which is a "gray ingredient" in the paleo diet and has been adopted by many that follow a paleo lifestyle. As always, choose organic meat.

2 lb. (900 g) **beef roast** (trimmed of fat)
½ **red onion** (diced)
1 inch fresh **ginger root**
2 tbs **sesame seeds**
10 **garlic cloves**
2 **jalapeños** (optional, diced)
2 tbs **balsamic vinegar** (optional)
6 **paleo tortillas** from recipe 9a

For the Slaw:
¼ cup **red onion** (diced)
½ **Jicama** (diced)
1 tsp **Asian dressing** (or other)
2 **limes**

Makes 6 servings
Calories: 210 per serving

Combine the red onion, ginger, sesame seeds, optional vinegar, jalapeños, garlic and beef in a slow cooker. Cover and cook for 9 hours in low heat.

Shred the beef using two forks.

Make the jicama slaw by combining the ingredients in the 2nd list. Stir to combine and serve on top of the tortillas.

Serve both and enjoy!

13. Italian Tomato Meatballs

Most meatballs combine pork, beef and veal. This recipe uses a lighter sauce to intensify the flavor without adding much on calories and fat. As always, choose organic meat.

1 **egg**
1 tsp **salt**
1 **small onion** (minced)
6 **garlic cloves** (minced)
1 lb. (450 g) **lean ground beef**
½ tbs **olive oil** or **coconut oil**
14 oz. (400 g) **dice tomatoes**
2 tsp **Italian seasoning**
1 **bay leaf**
1 **egg white**
¼ **parsley** (minced)
2 lb. (900 g) **chicken** or **turkey sausage**
28 oz. (800g) **tomatoes** (crushed)
1 tsp **red pepper flakes**
1 cup **chicken broth**

Makes 8 servings
Calories: 210 per serving

Whisk the egg and egg white together in a bowl. Add the parsley, garlic cloves and ¼ of the onion.

Combine the beef and sausage and stir to mix.

Roll the mixture into balls. The mixture should be enough for 22-25 meatballs, depending on the size you make them. Add to a slow cooker.

Heat the oil of your choice in a pan over medium heat. Sauté the remaining ¾ of the onion for 5 minutes until fragrant and tender.

Add the red pepper flakes, Italian seasoning, and garlic. Stir for 30 seconds before adding the diced tomatoes, bay leaf, crushed tomatoes and chicken broth.

Pour the sauce over the meatballs in the slow cooker and cook for 6 hours in low heat.

Enjoy!

14. Chicken and Cauliflower

This is a delicious Indian chicken dish filled with many flavors. As always, choose organic meat.

1 lb. (450 g) **chicken breast** (cut into chunks)
1 tbs **coriander**
1 tsp **salt**
2 whole **jalapeños**
1 **onion** (diced)
1 tbs **pepper**
3 inch (7.6 cm) **ginger** (grated)
1 tbs **arrowroot flour** or **coconut flour**
1 lb. (450 g) **chicken thighs**
1 tbs **cumin**
2 tbs **coconut butter**
6 **garlic cloves** (minced)
3 tbs **garam masala**
4 cups **tomatoes** (crushed)
1 lb. (450 g) **cauliflower florets**
1 cup nonfat **coconut milk**

Makes 10 servings
Calories: 200 per serving

Season the chicken with the cumin, salt, and coriander. Place at the bottom of a slow cooker. Add the jalapeños on top of the chicken.

Melt the coconut butter in a pan over medium heat. Add garlic and onion. Fry for 6 minutes or until fragrant and brown. Add the garam masala and ginger. Stir to combine.

Add the tomatoes to the slow cooker and pour the sauce over the chicken. Set heat to low and cook for 6 hours until the chicken is tender.

Add the cauliflower 1 hour before the chicken is done. Stir in the flour of your choice and coconut milk.

Cover for 10 minutes until the sauce is thick.

Enjoy!

15. Garlic Chicken

This garlic chicken recipe is easy to prepare using common ingredients. As always, choose organic meat.

2 lb. (900 g) **boneless chicken breast** (cut into chunks)
¾ tsp **dried basil**
1/3 cup paleo **ketchup** (optionally self-made)
Pinch of **red pepper flakes**
3 **garlic cloves** (minced)
1/3 cup **paleo sauce** of your choice (optional)

Makes 8 servings
Calories: 180 per serving

Add the garlic, optional sauce, paleo ketchup and basil in a bowl. Add the chicken into the bottom of the pot and pour the mixture over.

Cook for 4 hours in low heat. Add water if the chicken seems to be drying.

Place the chicken in a baking sheet, then broil for 5 minutes to crisp the outside.

Enjoy!

16. Thai Curry Beef

The combination of coconut milk and curry makes this dish interesting and delicious. It goes well with cauliflower rice or cabbage leaves. As always, choose organic meat.

1 lb. (450 g) **lean ground beef**
2 **garlic cloves** (minced)
1 tsp **red curry paste**
1 tsp **lime zest**
½ cup **coconut milk**
1 **medium leek** (sliced)
1 tsp **ginger** (minced)
1 ½ cup **tomato sauce**
2 tsp **lime juice**

Makes 4 servings
Calories: 220 per serving

Brown the ground beef in a pan, then add it to a slow cooker with garlic, red curry paste, lime, tomato sauce and leek. Cover and cook for 4 hours on high heat.

Stir in the lime juice and coconut milk. Cook for 15 more minutes before serving.

Enjoy!

17. Beef and Tomatoes

This is a delicious meal that can be paired with paleo noodles, the paleo zucchini noodles from section 1, or cauliflower rice from section 1. The tomato sauce and beef blends very well to create a delicious sauce. As always, choose organic meat.

2.5 lb. (1.1 kg) **lean beef chuck**
½ **onion** (diced)
4 **garlic cloves** (minced)
15 oz. (425 g) **tomatoes** (crushed)
15 oz. (425 g) **tomatoes** (diced)
2 tbs **thyme** (chopped)
2 tbs **rosemary** (minced)
1 **celery** (diced)
1 **carrot** (peeled, diced)
2 **bay leaves**

Makes 10 servings
Calories: 170 per serving

Combine the celery, onion, garlic and carrots in a slow cooker and season with salt and pepper.

Add the remaining ingredients and stir to mix.

Cover, set heat to low and cook for 6 hours or until the meat is tender.

Enjoy!

18. Coconut Chicken

This recipe is rich in ingredients, taste and health benefits. As always, choose organic meat.

2 lb. (900 g) **chicken breast** (cubed)
1 **shallot** (finely chopped)
2 tbs **coconut butter**
4 **garlic cloves** (minced)
2 tsp **garam masala**
1 tsp **cumin** (ground)
¾ cup **coconut milk**
2 ¼ tsp **cayenne peppers**
1 pinch **black pepper**
1 tbs **coconut oil**
¼ **white onion** (chopped)
2 tsp **lemon juice**
1 inch (2.5 cm) **ginger** (minced)
1 tsp **chili powder**
1 **bay leaf**
1 cup **tomato sauce**
1 pinch **salt**

Makes 6 servings
Calories: 240 per serving

Combine the shallots, onion, garlic, garam masala, chili powder, cumin, cayenne, bay leaf, lemon juice, tomato sauce and ginger in a blender and blend until smooth.

Combine the chicken breast, salt, paper, coconut oil, coconut butter and blended mix in a slow cooker. Cover, set heat to low and cook for 4 hours.

Taste and adjust the seasoning as needed.

19. Apple Rosemary Pork

This is a very satisfying dish that combines the taste of apples and pork. It ranks among my personal favorite meals. Choose coconut oil over olive oil for the most health benefits and remember to use organic meat.

3 lbs. (1.36 kg) **pork roast**
2 **apples** (peeled, cored, chopped)
1 tbs fresh **rosemary**
2 tbs **olive oil** or **coconut oil**
1 **onion** (chopped)
2 cloves **garlic** (crushed)
2 cups of **apple cider**
1 tsp minced fresh **thyme**
Salt and ground **pepper**

Makes 6 servings
Calories: 220 per serving

Heat the oil of your choice in a pan over medium heat. Add the pork and cook for 10 minutes until browned.

Transfer to a slow cooker, saving some of the oil. Place the onion in the pan, then cook for 5 minutes in the saved oil. Add the apples and garlic to the pan and cook for 5 more minutes. Transfer to the slow cooker.

Add the rest of the ingredients in the slow cooker. Cover, set heat to low and cook for 7 hours.

Taste and season with salt and pepper as needed.

Enjoy!

20. Chicken Family Dinner

This slow cooker chicken recipe is perfect for a family dinner or get-together. It is tender and full of flavor. Remember to use organic meat.

3 lb. (1.36 kg) **skinless chicken thighs**
2 **celery stalks** (chopped)
12 oz. (340 g) **tomatoes** (diced)
1 **red** or **green pepper** (chopped)
2 tsp **oregano**
2 tsp **salt**
1 tsp **red pepper flakes**
1 large **white onion** (sliced)
6 oz. (170 g) **tomato paste**
1 lb. (450 g) **mushrooms** (sliced)
6 **garlic cloves** (minced)
1 ½ tsp **basil** (dried)

Makes 11 servings
Calories: 215 per serving

Combine all of the ingredients in a bowl except for the chicken, onion and celery.

Layer the celery and onions in a slow cooker.

Season the chicken thighs with salt and pepper. Place on top of the celery and onions.

Pour the mixture in the bowl on top. Cover, set heat to low and cook for 8 hours.

This dish tends to taste better the next day.

Enjoy!

Section 3: Soups and Stews

1. Bacon Coconut Soup

Potato soup is a classic and needs no introduction. As always, remember to use organic meat.

3 bacon slices
3 lbs. (1.36 kg) **sweet potatoes** (peeled, sliced)
½ cup **water**
½ tsp **salt**
2 cups **coconut milk**
½ cup **coconut cream**
1 cup **onion** (chopped)
30 oz. (850 g) **chicken broth**
½ tsp **black pepper** (ground)
4 tsp **fresh chives** (chopped)

Makes 8 servings
Calories: 235 per serving

Cook the bacon in a large pan until crispy. Transfer to a plate and reserve about 2 tbs of liquid in the pan. Crumble the bacon. Add onions to the pan and sauté for 3 minutes.

Combine the onion, potato slices, chicken broth, salt, pepper and ½ cup of water in a slow cooker. Cover and cook for 8 hours on low heat until the potatoes are tender.

Mash the soup and add the coconut milk.

Set the heat to high and cook for another 20 minutes.

Ladle into soup bowls. Top with coconut cream. Sprinkle with chives and bacon.

Enjoy!

2. French Sausage Cassoulet

A cassoulet is a slow cooked casserole from the south of France. This one contains bacon and sausage flavors. Remember to use organic meat.

2 **bacon slices**
1 tsp **dried thyme**
3 **garlic cloves** (minced)
½ tsp **black pepper** (ground)
15 oz. (425 g) **mushrooms** (chopped)
15 oz. (425 g) **cauliflower rice**
8 oz. **sausage**
8 tsp **fresh leaf parsley** (chopped)
2 cups **onion** (chopped)
½ tsp **rosemary** (dried)
½ tsp **salt**
30 oz. (850 g) **tomatoes** (diced)
16 oz. **lean boneless pork loin** (cubed)

Makes 8 servings
Calories: 220 per serving

Cook the bacon in a skillet over medium heat until brown and crispy. Remove the bacon and crumble, then set aside to cool.

Add the thyme, garlic, rosemary and onion in a pan. Cook for about 3 minutes, until tender and fragrant.

Add the crumbled bacon, pepper, salt and tomatoes and bring to a boil. Remove from heat. Add the mushrooms, cauliflower rice, sausage and pork. Stir to combine. Put the mixture into the slow cooker and top with tomatoes.

Repeat the layers and cook for 5 hours in low heat. Ladle into soup bowls. Sprinkle with parsley.

3. Paleo Pozole

Pozole (aka posole) is a well-known Mexican soup or stew. The spicy flavor from the chilies make this dish perfect for cold weather. This version of Pazole eliminates the chicken and corn that is normally added to it. Instead, we use cauliflower rice, which is no grain and suitable for the paleo diet.

8 cups **vegetable broth**
2 **jalapeños** (seeded)
Salt and **pepper** to taste
4 **garlic cloves**
1 tbs dried **oregano**
3 **zucchini** (chopped)
2 **poblano peppers**
1 lb. (450 g) **tomatillos**
1 small bunch **cilantro**
60 oz. (1.7 kg) **cauliflower rice**
For garnish:
Shredded **cabbage**, **radishes**, **lime**, **jalapeños** or **avocado**

Makes 8 servings
Calories: 210 per serving

Combine the cilantro, cauliflower rice, tomatillos, peppers, oregano, salt, pepper, garlic and cilantro in a blender.

Pour the vegetable broth and blend until smooth. Taste and adjust the seasoning as necessary.

Pour the mixture in a slow cooker and cook for 4 hours on high heat. Add the zucchini and continue to cook for 30 minutes.

Ladle into soup bowls and use the garnish of your choice.

This dish can be served with baked sweet potatoes, cabbage and lime juice.

4. Cauliflower Soup

This healthy soup is packed with vegetables and rich in taste.

1 **cauliflower head** (cut into florets)
1 **onion** (diced)
2 **garlic cloves** (diced)
¼ cup **arrowroot flour** or **coconut flour**
1 cup **coconut milk**
1 cup **carrots** (diced)
3 **celery stalks**
4 cups **vegetable broth**
Salt and **pepper**

Makes 8 servings
Calories: 200 calories per serving

Combine the carrots, celery, cauliflower, garlic and broth in a slow cooker. Cook for 4 hours in low heat until the vegetables are tender.

Stir in the coconut milk. Add the flour of your choice and increase to medium heat. Cook for 1 more hour until the soup thickens.

Season the soup with salt and pepper. Use the blender to process the soup.

Enjoy

5. Traditional Mexican Beef Stew

This recipe combines traditional beef stew with spices like chili powder and chipotle peppers. As always, choose organic meat from free range animals. This recipe contains cocoa, an ingredient in dark bitter chocolate that is healthy and contains a lot of antioxidants. It is fine for the paleo diet.

1/3 cup **arrowroot flour** or **coconut flour**
1 tbs **ancho chili pepper** (ground)
1 tbs **coconut butter**
¼ tsp **black pepper** (ground)
1 red **bell pepper** (chopped)
14 oz. (400) **tomatoes** (diced)
1 tbs **unsweetened cocoa**
2 **beef briskets** (trimmed fat)
½ tsp **salt**
1 **green bell pepper** (chopped)
1 **yellow onion** (chopped)
1 ½ cups **beef broth**
1 tbs **adobo sauce**

Makes 7 servings
Calories: 200 per serving

Combine the ancho chili, salt, pepper, flour and cocoa in a small bowl. Coat the beef brisket in the flour of your choice and set aside.

Heat the coconut butter in a slow cooker and brown the brisket on each side. Transfer to plate and set aside.

Add the onion and pepper to the cooker. Cook for 5 minutes until the onions are fragrant and tender.

Add the beef broth, chipotle sauce, pepper, flour and tomatoes. Stir to combine.

Bring to a simmer and return the brisket to the slow cooker. Cook for 3 hours on high heat until the meat is tender.

Use forks to shred the meat into pieces.

Adjust the seasoning as needed and add chipotle sauce.

Enjoy!

6. Sweet Potato Sausage Stew

This lentil stew has a spicy taste, combining a jalapeño with sweet potatoes and spinach. It goes very well with eggs.

1/3 lb. (150 g) **chicken sausage**
1 **celery** (chopped)
1 **sweet potato** (chopped)
3 cups **spinach**
½ tsp **cumin**
2 tbs **tomato paste**
¼ tsp **salt**
4 cups **chicken broth**
½ **onion** (diced)
1 **carrot** (chopped)
1 cup dry **lentils**
1 **jalapeño**
1 **garlic cloves** (minced)
1 **thyme sprigs**
¼ tsp **pepper**

Makes 5 servings
Calories: 150 calories per serving

Fry the chicken sausage until brown, then drain the fat. Place in a slow cooker.

Add the remaining ingredients to the cooker and cook for 5 hours on low heat.

Taste and season with salt and pepper.

You can store this dish in an airtight container and freeze it for about a week.

Enjoy

7. Brazilian Chicken Stew

This Brazilian dish is perfect for cold weather. It can be served as is or on top of cauliflower rice.

1 ½ cups **low salt chicken broth**
1 lb. (450 g) **skinless chicken breast**
6 **garlic cloves**
½ cup **water**
7 oz. (225 g) **onion** (chopped)
1 **green** bell **pepper** (chopped)
6 **skinless boneless chicken thighs**
4 cups **cilantro leaves** (chopped)
2 large **jalapeños** (seeded)
1 **red bell pepper** (chopped)
1 lb. (450 g) **sweet potatoes** (peeled, chopped)
1 tsp **cumin** (ground)
Salt and **pepper** (ground)

Makes 7 servings
Calories: 220 per serving

Combine the water, cilantro, garlic, onion, salt, pepper, red pepper, green pepper, cumin and jalapeños in a blender, then blend until smooth.

Pour the mixture into a slow cooker and add the chicken. Cook for 2 hours on high heat until the meat is cooked through.

Add the broth until the sauce thickens. Taste and adjust the seasoning with salt and pepper as needed.

Add the potatoes to the slow cooker and make sure that everything is submerged in the sauce. Cover and cook for 45 minutes on high heat until the potatoes are cooked through.

8. Beefy Stew

This is a healthier version of the traditional stew. Cooking a stew in a slow cooker is easy and you can use any combination of vegetables for this dish. As always, choose organic meat to make it healthy.

1 ½ lb. (680 g) **lean beef** (cut into chunks)
½ lb. (225 g) **parsnips** (chopped)
3 **celery ribs** (chopped)
2 tbs **Worcestershire sauce**
2 cups **water**
2 **bay leaves**
1 tsp **paprika**
2 tbs **arrowroot flour** or **coconut flour**
1 tsp **salt**
½ tsp **pepper**
¼ tsp **allspice** (ground)
2 cups fat free **beef broth**

Makes 8 servings
Calories: 232 per serving

Heat the oil in a slow cooker over medium heat. Add the beef and brown on all sides.

Add water, garlic, bay leaves, smoked paprika, Worcestershire sauce and onion. Let it simmer for 90 minutes.

Add the parsnips, celery, potato, carrots, and broth. Cook for 1 hour or until the meat is tender and can be shredded easily. The total cooking time will largely depend on the size of the beef you are using.

Mix the flour of your choice with water and stir to combine. Pour into the stew and bring to a boil.

Remove from heat and set aside before serving. This stew tastes best after storing it for two days, so consider preparing it in advance.

Enjoy!

9. Chicken Paleo-Noodle Soup

Chicken noodle soup is a classic favorite in many families. However, we need to substitute regular pasta with the paleo noodles or paleo zucchini noodles from section 1. Remember to use organic meat.

1 tbs **olive oil** or **coconut oil**
1 ½ lbs. **skinless, boneless chicken breast** or **thighs**
2 **cups onion** (chopped)
1 tbs **rosemary**
8 oz. (225 g) **mushrooms** (pre-sliced)
6 oz. (170 g) package **baby spinach**
½ tsp fresh **black pepper** (ground)
1 ½ lbs. (680 g) **skinless chicken thighs**
1 tsp **salt**
6 cups **chicken broth**
1 cup **celery** (chopped)
10 oz. (280 g) **carrot** (shredded)
1/3 cup **parsley** (chopped)
¼ cup **lemon juice**
4 cups **paleo noodles** or **Zucchini noodles**

Makes 11 servings
Calories: 250 per serving

Combine the oil, ½ tsp of salt and paleo noodles of your choice in a large bowl, then toss to coat.

Mix the chicken broth, chicken breast, onion, celery, rosemary, carrots, mushrooms, parsley, spinach and the remaining ½ tsp of salt in a slow cooker. Bring to a boil and simmer for 25-30 minutes.

Remove the chicken, set aside and allow to cool. Shred using a fork.

Add the carrots and mushroom to the cooker. Reduce the heat and cook until the carrots are tender.

Add the parsley, shredded chicken and spinach. Cook until the spinach wilts.

Add the paleo noodles, lemon juice and pepper. Cook for 10 more minute.

Enjoy!

10. Vegetarian Spinach Stew

This stew is rich in vegetables, protein, and fiber. It is also a great vegetarian meal, but if you want to have a meat friendly dish, you can serve it with chicken as well.

4 **garlic cloves** (chopped)
1 ½ cups **tomato sauce**
1 tbs **coriander** (ground)
1 tsp **salt**
1 ½ cups (350 ml) **coconut milk**
2 tbs **ginger** (minced)
1 tbs **garam masala**
1 tbs **cumin** (ground)
1/8 tsp **cayenne pepper**
30 oz. (850 g) **thawed spinach**

Makes 8 servings
Calories: 201 per serving

Add all ingredients except for the spinach in a slow cooker. Cover and cook for 3 hours on high heat.

Wash and drain the spinach. Add to the cooker and cook for 1 more hour.

This dish goes well with cauliflower rice or baked sweet potatoes.

Enjoy!

Section 4: Appetizers and Side Dishes

1. Pepper Mushrooms in Bouillon

This spicy recipe is rich in taste and easy to prepare. It works very well as a side dish for sweet potatoes.

½ lb. (225 g) **mushrooms**
1 **red bell pepper** (chopped)
3 oz. (85 g) **pepperoni slices**
1 **chicken bouillon cube**
¼ tsp **red pepper** (ground)
1 ½ cups **cauliflower rice**
4 **green onions** (chopped)
1 **jalapeño pepper** (diced)
2 cups **hot water**
½ tsp **salt**
15 oz. (425 g) **Mexican stewed tomatoes**

Makes 12 servings
Calories: 200 per serving

Combine all of the ingredients except for the tomatoes and cauliflower rice in a slow cooker. Cover and cook for 8 hours in low heat.

Add the cauliflower rice and tomatoes. Cover and cook for another 30 minutes.

Enjoy!

2. Paleo Bolognese

This classic Italian dish needs no introduction. To conform to the paleo diet, we need to serve it with paleo noodles or paleo zucchini noodles from section 1 instead of pasta. Use organic meat.

1 ¾ **cups onion** (chopped)
½ cup **carrots** (chopped)
8 oz. (225 g) **beef** (ground)
8 oz. (225 g) **veal** (ground)
¼ cup **parsley** (chopped)
1 tsp **black pepper** (ground)
¼ tsp **cinnamon** (ground)
1 **bay leaf**
2/3 cup **celery** (chopped)
6 **garlic cloves** (minced)
8 oz. (225 g) **lean pork** (ground)
1 ½ cups **tomatoes** (crushed)
1 cup **beef broth**
2 tbs **tomato paste**
1 tsp **thyme** (dried)
½ tsp **oregano** (dried)
¼ tsp **salt**

Makes 6 servings
Calories: 235 per serving

Add the carrot, celery, onion and garlic in a pan, then sauté for 4 minutes over medium heat.

Add the veal, beef and pork. Coat with the vegetable mixture. Sauté for a few more minutes until the meat is browned. Stir the mixture to crumble.

Remove the meat and place in a slow cooker.

Add the tomatoes and the remaining ingredients. Cook for 8 hours in low heat, then remove the bay leaf. Before it is done, prepare the paleo noodles of your choice.

This dish can be stored in the freezer for a week.

Enjoy!

3. Bacon with Collard Greens

This dish can be a great appetizer or side dish to pork or mashed sweet potatoes. This recipe contains the option to include some vinegar, which is a "gray ingredient" in the paleo diet and has been adopted by many that follow a paleo lifestyle.

3 **bacon slices**
16 oz. (450) **collard greens** (chopped)
2 **garlic cloves** (minced)
1 ½ cups (350 ml) **chicken broth**
1 cup **onion** (chopped)
¼ tsp **salt**
1 **bay leaf**
3 tbs **balsamic vinegar** (optional)

Makes 5 servings
Calories: 80 per serving

Cook the bacon in a frying pan until crispy. Transfer to a plate and crumble.

Add onions and sauté for 5 minutes until fragrant and soft.

Add the collard greens and cook until the vegetables are starting to wilt. Stir occasionally.

Remove the collard greens and put them in a bowl, then combine the salt, garlic cloves, bay leaf and chicken broth in a slow cooker. Cover and cook for 4 hours in low heat.

Add the optional vinegar to the greens before serving with bacon.

Enjoy!

4. Sweet Potato Vegetable Dish

This is a delicious side dish that can be topped with crumbled bacon. This recipe contains the option to include some vinegar, which is a "gray ingredient" in the paleo diet and has been adopted by many that follow a paleo lifestyle. Remember to use organic meat.

1 ½ lb. (680 g) **sweet potatoes**
1 lb. **carrots**
¾ cup **cranberries** (dried)
3 tbs **olive oil** or **coconut oil**
1 tsp **salt**
1/3 cup **flat leaf parsley** (chopped)
1 lb. (450 g) **parsnips**
2 large **red onions** (chopped)
2 tbs **balsamic vinegar** (optional)
½ tsp **pepper** (ground)

Makes 6 servings
Calories: 180 per serving

Combine the onions, carrots, parsnips and cranberries in a slow cooker. Make sure to layer the sweet potatoes on top.

Whisk the oil of your choice, optional balsamic vinegar, salt and ground pepper in a bowl and pour on top of the vegetables.

Cover and cook for 4 hours in low heat until the vegetables are tender.

Sprinkle with the parsley before serving.

Enjoy!

5. Sausage and Apple Stuffing

This stuffing is perfect for thanksgiving. We have been using it in our family for several years. Remember to use organic meat for maximum health benefits. Instead of the cauliflower rice, you can also use paleo bread crumbs. There are many paleo breads to choose from.

8 oz. (425 g) **pork sausage**, (browned, drained)
5 cups **mushrooms**
3 cups **cauliflower rice**
1 1/2 tsp **sage** (rubbed)
1/2 tsp **black pepper**
1/2 cup **chicken broth**
1 1/2 cups **celery** (diced)
3 tbs **coconut butter** (melted)
1 1/2 cups **onion** (chopped)
1 1/2 cups **apples** (chopped)
1 tsp **salt**

Makes 8 servings
Calories: 267 per serving

Heat the coconut butter in a slow cooker on low heat. Add the sausage to the cooker and brown it.

Add the vegetables, apples, cauliflower rice, mushrooms, seasonings, and ½ cup chicken broth. Stir to coat.

Cover, set heat on high and cook for 2 ½ to 3 hours.

If you need more moisture, you can add an extra ¼ cup of broth before serving. Stir to mix.

Enjoy!

6. Zucchini Dish

This dish combines many flavors, ranging from the exotic quality of coconuts to the tanginess of herbs.

2 zucchinis
5 cups (1.2 liters) **chicken broth**
½ cup **shallots** (chopped)
1 tsp **oregano** (crushed, dried)
3 tbs **coconut butter**
1 tbs **olive oil** or **coconut oil**
1 **yellow sweet pepper** (chopped)
2 cups **cauliflower rice**
3 **garlic cloves** (minced)
3 cups **mushrooms** (sliced)
Italian flat leaf parsley

Makes 12 servings
Calories: 205 per serving

Lightly coat the slow cooker with oil or cooking spray.

Add the zucchini, cauliflower rice, oregano, salt and pepper, chicken broth, garlic, and shallots. Cover and cook for 4 hours in high heat.

Add the coconut butter, then remove from heat. Set aside for 15 minutes. Pour the vegetable broth, if the dish is too dry.

Heat the oil of your choice in a pan. Cook the sliced mushrooms, then transfer to plate.

Top with sweet pepper and parsley.

Enjoy!

7. Sweet Potatoes and Bacon

This side dish is a different treat from the usual sweet potatoes. Instead, use herbs to add more flavor to the dish. As always, use organic meat.

4 lb. (1.8 kg) **sweet potatoes** (peeled, sliced)
2 tbs **coconut oil** (optional)
½ tsp **dried leaf sage** (crushed)
2 tbs **coconut butter**
½ cup **orange concentrate**
1 ½ tsp **salt**
½ tsp **dried thyme**
4 **crispy bacon slices**

Makes 9 servings
Calories: 180 per serving

Place the sweet potatoes in a slow cooker.

Mix the orange concentrate, optional coconut oil, sage, thyme and salt in a bowl.

Pour the mixture over the sweet potatoes and toss to coat. Add the coconut butter.

Cook in low heat for 6 hours.

Sprinkle with crumbled bacon before serving.

Enjoy!

8. Sweet Potato Ginger Dish

This side dish is a personal favorite. It combines health and sweetness, containing no sugars and few calories. Specifically, this dish is great in winter and around Christmas time.

2 **Granny Smith apples** (peeled, chopped)
1 ½ lb. (680 g) **sweet potatoes** (peeled, cut)
2 tbs **cranberries** (dried)
1/2 cup **water**
1/8 tsp **black pepper** (ground)
1 1/2 tsp **fresh ginger** (grated)
1/2 tsp **salt**
1/4 tsp **nutmeg** (ground)
1/4 cup **coconut oil** (melted)
1/2 tsp **cinnamon** (ground)

Makes 8 servings
Calories: 103 per serving

Combine the sweet potatoes, cranberries, apples, cinnamon, ginger, salt, nutmeg and pepper in a slow cooker. Stir to combine. Add water and coconut oil.

Cover and cook on low heat for 5 ½ hours, or 2 ½ hours on high heat.

Enjoy!

9. Barley Squash Spinach

This dish is easy to make and very nutritious without loading up on calories. Squash in particular provides many important vitamins.

2 lb. (910 g) **butternut squash** (peeled, cubed)
1 **medium onion** (cut into wedges)
1 ¾ cups (410 ml) **vegetables broth**
3 **garlic cloves** (minced)
¼ tsp **black pepper** (ground)
10 oz. (280 g) **spinach** (chopped)
1 cup **barley**
½ cup **water**
¾ tsp **salt**

Makes 6 servings
Calories: 162 per serving

Place the squash, spinach, broth, water, onion, barley, garlic, salt and pepper in a slow cooker.

Cover and cook for 7 hours in low heat, or 3 hours in high heat.

Remove and let it sit for 10 minutes before serving.

Enjoy!

10. Broccoli and Cauliflower in Sauce

This recipe provides a wonderful blend of Alfredo sauce and coconut oil. The herbs add a delicious flavor to the dish.

4 cups **broccoli florets**
14 oz. (400 ml) **Alfredo sauce**
1 **large onion** (chopped)
¼ tsp **black pepper** (ground)
4 cups **cauliflower florets**
10 tbs **coconut oil**
1 tsp **thyme** (dried)
½ cup **almonds** (sliced)

Makes 10 servings
Calories: 170 calories per serving

Place the cauliflower, broccoli, coconut oil, onion, pasta sauce, thyme and pepper in a small slow cooker.

Cook for 7 hours in low heat or 3 hours in high heat.

Stir occasionally. Adjust the seasoning as desired and sprinkle with almonds.

Enjoy!

11. Sweet Potatoes in Broth

Mashed potatoes are easy to make and is one of the classic side dishes that can be served with any meal.

3 lb. (1.36 kg) **sweet potatoes** (peeled)
1 **bay leaf**
1 cup **coconut milk**
1 tsp **salt**
6 **garlic cloves** (halved)
3 ¼ cups (770 ml) **chicken broth**
¼ cup **coconut butter**
Fresh **black pepper** (ground)

Makes 11 servings
Calories: 130 per serving

Place the sweet potatoes, garlic and bay leaf in a slow cooker. Add the broth.

Cover, set heat to low and cook for 4 hours.

Drain the potatoes in a colander. Catch the cooking liquid in a bowl below, then remove the bay leaf and discard it.

Return the potatoes to the slow cooker. Mash using a fork or a masher.

Combine the coconut milk and coconut butter in a saucepan. Heat until the butter melts. Add the coconut milk mixture to the slow cooker and return some of the cooking liquid until desired consistency is reached.

Transfer to a bowl, sprinkle with ground pepper and garnish with bay leaves.

Enjoy!

12. Cabbage with Apples

This is a wonderful and simple side dish that adds an apple taste to any meal. It works very well with chicken.

1 medium-sized **cabbage** (chopped)
2 **tart apples** (diced)
1 tbs **olive oil** or **coconut oil**
3 tbs **spicy mustard**
1 cup **apple juice**
1 **onion** (quartered, sliced)
1/2 cup **chicken broth**
½ tsp **salt**
1/8 tsp **pepper** (ground)

Makes 7 servings
Calories: 87 per serving

Heat the oil of your choice in a slow cooker over low heat. Add the cabbage, apples, onion, and season with salt and pepper. Stir to mix.

Combine the chicken broth, mustard, and apple juice in a bowl. Whisk to combine. Add the mixture to the cooker.

Cover and cook for 7 hours in low heat. Stir every 2 hours.

With a slotted spoon, remove from the cooker to a bowl or plates.

Enjoy!

13. Carrot Garlic Soup

This carrot garlic soup provides a delicious and healthy meal for the whole family. Remember to use organic meat.

2 lb. (910 g) **carrots**
3 **garlic cloves** (finely chopped)
1 tsp **curry powder**
½ cup **coconut cream**
8 oz. (225 g) **shrimps** (peeled, cooked)
6 **white and green scallions**
2 tbs **fresh ginger** (chopped)
2 ½ cups low sodium **chicken broth**
1 pinch **salt**
Cilantro to sprinkle (optional)

Makes 6 servings
Calories: 177 per serving

Combine the scallions, ginger, curry powder, garlic and carrots in a slow cooker.

Add 2 cups of water, then bring to a boil. Cook for 7 to 8 hours in low heat until carrots are tender.

Remove from heat and allow to cool slightly.

Puree the soup in batches, then return to the slow cooker.

Add the coconut cream and season with salt until completely heated through.

Ladle the soup into bowls and top with optional cilantro.

Enjoy!

14. Acorn Squash Stew

This is a slow cooker soup made from chicken broth and squash. As always, use organic meat and coconut options for maximum health benefits.

3 cups **cauliflower rice**
2 **chicken breasts** (diced)
1 cube **vegetable bouillon**
2 tbs **pesto**
1 **onion** (diced)
4 tbs **coconut cream**
1 **thyme** (chopped)
1 **acorn squash**
1 ½ cups (350 ml) **chicken broth**
1 tbs **garlic** (minced)
4 cups **water**
1 fresh **sage**
1 **basil** (chopped)

Makes 6 servings
Calories: 138 per serving

Cut the squash in half then bake at high heat. Bake until tender.

Prepare the cauliflower rice. Set aside.

Place all of the ingredients in a slow cooker except for the coconut cream.

Cook for about 12 hours. Add water, if the mixture starts to dry out.

Add the coconut cream and season it with salt before serving.

Enjoy!

15. Coconut Mushrooms and Cauliflower

This is a delicious coconut recipe, healthy and very easy to prepare.

1 cup **mushrooms**
1 **onion** (large, finely diced)
14 oz. (400 ml) **coconut milk**
2 **cloves garlic** (minced)
1 tsp **red pepper flakes**
3 cups **chicken broth**
1 ½ cups **cauliflower rice**
½ tsp **salt**

Makes 8 servings
Calories: 228 per serving

Combine the mushrooms, red pepper flakes, onion, garlic, coconut milk and chicken broth in a slow cooker.

Stir in cauliflower rice and salt. Cover and cook on low heat for 9hours until everything is tender.

Enjoy!

Book 2: Paleo Baking Recipes

Preamble: Is this Paleo?

All ingredients used in this book are either paleo or commonly considered to be acceptable for the paleo diet. The latter means that most people agree with it, while only a minority disagrees. Each ingredient has been rigorously checked to ensure this fact, but as you know, there are rare cases where opinions diverge.

If you spot an ingredient that you personally do not consider paleo, feel free to replace it as you see fit. Better yet, check appropriate paleo ingredient lists on the Internet to see for yourself whether an ingredient you are unsure about is okay.

The purpose of this recipe book is to replace the usual ingredients for pastries with paleo alternatives, including paleo chocolate, paleo cheese, and natural sugars. Since pastries use at least *some* ingredients that are rarely used in cooking, you may be unfamiliar with their paleoness, so let us have a quick look at a few of them.

Raisins

Raisins are just grapes that are sun-dried or dehydrated. They are natural foods without additives or added sugar. However, they are high in natural sugars and have lots of calories, so they should not be over eaten.

Chocolate (cocoa)

Chocolate is made from cocoa, a natural ingredient that itself is paleo. Dark chocolate is paleo as well, because it contains very high amounts of cocoa. Milk chocolate, on the other hand, is likely not to be considered paleo, but opinions vary on this matter.

As you will see in the first recipe of this book, paleo chocolate can easily be home made from coconut milk and cocoa powder.

Coconut

Coconut ingredients of any kind (milk, butter, oil, flour, powder, sugar) are healthy and natural. In fact, they are eaten in very large amounts by indigenous islanders in the pacific, who are known to be the healthiest people in the world. People in tropical places like this have been eating coconuts for thousands of years. This provides a tremendous opportunity for paleo dieters, since so many ingredients are made from coconut. You can bake with coconut flour, use coconut sugar to sweeten pastries, make chocolate with coconut milk and grease pans with coconut oil.

Vanilla extract

Vanilla is an orchid that grows in Africa, where humans originally came from. This means that vanilla has always been readily available to our species.

Judging from the literature out there, vanilla extract is regarded as a paleo ingredient, even though it contains alcohol. Since it is concentrated, you will be using such small amounts of it (like ½ tsp) that it does not even matter to the biochemistry of your body and can be ignored.

Pumpkin Pie Spice

This is paleo, simply because it is made from paleo ingredients, such as cinnamon and ginger.

Honey

Like any brown bear knows, honey is made by bees and readily available in nature, which makes it a telltale paleo food. In its raw form, it has many health benefits and comes with natural sugars that can serve as a replacement to white/brown sugar.

However, most honey available in supermarkets today has been processed at high temperatures and is devoid of most nutrients. Processed honey may or may not be paleo, as opinions vary in this case. The best way to go about it is to buy raw honey from a local farmer or to find an online store that sells bio-foods.

Cavemen had to work hard to find honey and did not have much available at any time, so make sure you do not eat it every day. For baking, we will need honey in small amounts to add sweetness and extra taste.

Section 1: Chocolate recipes

1. Dark Chocolate

Paleo chocolate made easy. There are many possible variations to this recipe, if you add orange zest, almond butter, dried coconut, chopped nuts, cinnamon, or other ingredients. The chocolate is ready in a little more than an hour.

½ cup **cocoa powder**
½ cup **coconut oil**
½ tsp **vanilla extract**
3 tbs **raw honey**
1 pinch of **sea salt**

Makes 8 servings
Calories: 139 per serving

In a pan, melt coconut oil over medium-low flame. Stir in cocoa, vanilla, honey and salt. Whisk to blend.

Pour the mixture into a candy mold or rimmed plastic tray. Refrigerate for an hour.

Enjoy!

2. Coco-Choco Cake

This is a simple yet satisfyingly dense chocolate cake that uses coconut ingredients. Top with your favorite frosting. It is ready in 45 minutes.

1 cup **coconut flour**
¾ tsp. **baking soda**
¾ cup **cocoa powder**
9 large pastured **eggs**
1 cup **raw honey**
¾ cup **coconut oil** (melted)
1 ½ tbs **vanilla extract**
¾ tsp. **salt**

Makes 24 servings
Calories: 145 per serving

Preheat oven to 350°F (180 °C).

In a bowl, combine flour, cocoa, salt and baking soda. Mix well.

In a separate bowl, beat eggs until fluffy. Add the rest of the ingredients and mix to blend. Slowly pour this mixture into the first bowl and mix until a batter is formed. Add water if needed to attain desired consistency.

The batter should be enough for 2 round cakes at 9 inches (23 cm). Fill 2 cake pans lined with parchment paper and bake for about 30 minutes, or until toothpick comes out clean when inserted at the center. Alternatively, use cupcake forms to make cupcakes.

Remove from oven and let cool on wire rack.

Enjoy!

3. Coconut-Almond Chocolate Cake

This is a two-layered chocolate cake with frosting. It is done in 45 minutes.

Cake:
½ cup **cocoa powder**
4 pastured **eggs**
1 cup **almond flour**
¼ cup **coconut flour**
½ cup **arrowroot powder**
1 tsp **baking soda**
1 cup **raw honey**
¼ cup **coconut oil**
2 tsp **vanilla extract**
½ tsp **salt**

Frosting:
¾ cup **dark chocolate chips**
    or self-made **paleo chocolate**
1 tbs **raw honey**
6 tbs **coconut milk**

Makes 16 slices
Calories: 266 per slice

Preheat oven to 350°F (180 °C) and grease two 9 inch (23 cm) springform pans. Line bottom with parchment paper.

In a bowl, combine dry ingredients. Whisk in wet ingredients and mix until desired consistency is attained. Transfer batter to the prepared pans and bake for about 30 minutes, or until a toothpick comes out clean when inserted at the center.

For the frosting: In a bowl, melt dark chocolate chips (or self-made paleo chocolate from recipe 1) over a hot water bath or in a double boiler, if you have one. Once melted, add coconut milk and honey, then whisk until smooth.

Remove from heat and let cool to room temperature. It may take ½ hour. Make sure the mixture does not get hard and can still be poured. Spread the frosting on top of one cake, followed by the second cake to create a two-layered cake. Alternatively, you can use the frosting to cover both cakes and serve them separately.

Enjoy!

4. Chocolate Applesauce Cake

This Paleo chocolate cake is baked in about 40 minutes.

5 pastured **eggs**
1 cup **applesauce**
¼ cup **raw honey**
1 tbs **vanilla extract**
¼ cup **coconut oil**
1/3 cup **coconut flour**
¾ cup + 2 tbs **cocoa powder**
1/3 cup **tapioca flour**
½ tsp. **baking soda**
½ tsp. **baking powder**
¼ tsp. **salt**

Makes 12 servings
Calories: 142 per serving

Preheat oven to 325°F (160°C). Lightly grease a Bundt cake pan. In bowl, whisk eggs using a hand mixer. Add the rest of the wet ingredients, ending with coconut oil. Set aside.

In another bowl, combine flour with the rest of the dry ingredients. Mix well. Slowly pour into the wet mixture and mix using hand mixer.

Drizzle cocoa powder all over the prepared Bundt pan. Shake to remove excess powder. Transfer batter into the pan and bake for about 40 minutes.

Remove from the oven allow to cool for 20 minutes. Run a knife around the edge of the pan to loosen the cake. Place a plate or wire rack over the pan and flip it over to remove the cake. Cool and cut into 12 slices.

5. Hot Chocolate with Coconut-Almond Milk

A thick and creamy hot chocolate treat for extra cold winter days. It can be used as a glazing for the cupcakes in recipe 5 of section 4.

1 cup **coconut milk**
2 cups **almond milk**
1 tsp **vanilla extract**
2 tbs **cocoa powder**
4 oz. (110g) **dark chocolate chips**
   or self-made **paleo chocolate**

Makes 4 servings
Calories: 126 per serving

In a medium sized pot, combine all ingredients but the chocolate. Heat over medium-low flame and mix to blend.

Add the dark chocolate chips or self-made paleo chocolate (from recipe 1). Simmer and constantly stir over low heat for about 2 minutes, or until fully blended. Serve hot.

Enjoy!

6. Paleo Mousse Chocolate

This recipe is a real treat and can be used for a wide variety of pastries. It is used in recipe 2 of section 6 for banana-chocolate ice cream.

1 cup **hazelnuts**
¼ cup **cocoa powder**
2 tbs **coconut oil**
½ cup **almond milk**
2 tbs **coconut sugar**
½ tsp **vanilla extract**

Makes: 1 cup
Calories: 120 per serving

Preheat oven to 350°F (180°C).

Line a baking sheet with parchment paper. Place hazelnuts on the sheet and roast for about 10 minutes. Remove and let cool. Remove hazelnut skins by bundling them in a kitchen towel and massing the bundle.

Transfer to a food processor and process to a smooth paste. Add all other ingredients for the chocolate cream and process the mixture until well blended. Transfer to an airtight container or glass jar and store it in the fridge.

Enjoy!

Section 2: Cake recipes

1. Coconut Almond Cake

A creamy cake with almond topping that is ready in 1 hour.

Batter:
1 cup **coconut flour**
1 tsp **cinnamon** (ground)
8 large pastured **eggs**
1 tsp **baking soda**
4 oz. (125 ml) **almond milk yoghurt**
5 tbs **coconut oil** (melted)
½ cup **raw honey**
1 tbs **vanilla extract**
½ tsp **sea salt**

Topping:
1 ½ cups **almonds**
2 tsp **cinnamon**
4 tbs **raw honey**
4 tbs **coconut oil** (cubed)

Makes 6 servings
Calories: 342 per serving

Preheat oven to 325°F (160°F) and place a rack in the middle. Lightly grease an 8 x 8 inch (20 x 20 cm) baking dish.

Place all batter ingredients into a food processor. Process until smooth. Transfer to the prepared baking dish. Clean the food processor and process the topping ingredients until almonds are coarsely chopped. Spread topping on the batter and bake for 45 minutes, or until golden brown. Remove and let cool.

2. Pumpkin Almond Cake

This luscious pumpkin cake is perfect for Halloween parties or Thanksgiving. It takes about 45 minutes to make.

The Cake:
1 cup **pumpkin puree**
2 large **pastured eggs**
1 cup **almond butter**
¼ cup **raw honey**
1 ½ tsp **baking powder**
1 tsp **vanilla extract**
1 tsp **cinnamon**
½ tsp **baking soda**
¼ tsp **cloves**
1 tsp **ground ginger**
¼ tsp **nutmeg**
½ tsp **lemon zest**

The Frosting:
1/3 cup **coconut butter**
½ cup **coconut oil**
½ tbs **raw honey**
1 tsp **vanilla extract**
10 **Almonds**

Makes 10 servings
Calories: 358 per serving

Preheat oven to 350°F (180°C). Grease an 8 inch (20 cm) baking dish.

In a bowl, combine all of the cake ingredients. Mix to blend. Transfer to the prepared baking dish and bake for about 30 minutes. Remove and let cool on a wire rack.

For the frosting: Place coconut butter and oil in a bowl and heat it over hot water or inside a microwave until softened, but not entirely melted. Add honey, and vanilla extract to the bowl and whisk with a hand mixer until fluffy.

Slice cake into 10 wedges. Spread frosting on top of each wedge and place an almond on it. Loosely cover with plastic wrap and chill.

Enjoy!

3. Layered Fruit Cake with Walnut Topping

A fruit cake with walnut and coconut topping. It is ready in 1 hour.

¾ cup + 2 tbs **coconut flour**
¼ cup + ½ cup **coconut butter**
Coconut oil (for greasing)
¾ cup **walnuts** (chopped)
¼ cup + 3 tbs **raw honey**
1 tsp **cinnamon**
1 medium **apple** (peeled, thinly sliced)
2 medium **pears** (peeled, thinly sliced)
2 tsp **lemon juice**
5 large **pastured eggs**
1 tsp **vanilla extract**
¼ cup **arrowroot** powder
¾ cup **coconut milk**
¾ tsp **baking** powder
½ tsp **baking** soda
½ tsp **sea salt**

Makes 12 servings
Calories: 292 per serving

Preheat the oven to 350 °F (180 °C). Grease a 9-inch (23 cm) springform pan with coconut oil and line it with foil.

In a bowl, combine cinnamon, walnuts, and honey. Set aside. In another small bowl, mix ¾ cup flour and ¼ cup butter until a crumbly mixture is attained. Fold in the walnut-cinnamon mixture from before and set aside.

In large bowl, combine fruits with the lemon juice. Set aside. In another bowl, combine remaining butter, honey, and eggs. Whisk until blended. Slowly add the remaining flour and the rest of the ingredients. Mixing after each addition until a batter is formed.

Spread half of the batter on the bottom of the pan. Layer the fruit mixture on the top. Spread the remaining batter over the fruit and top with the walnut-cinnamon mixture.

Bake for about 50 minutes, or until toothpick comes out clean if inserted at the center. Remove and let cool on a wire rack. Slice into 12 wedges and serve.

Enjoy!

4. Carrot Cake with Raisins

This cake is filled with ingredients that make it soft, healthy and give it a nice odor that fills your home with taste. It is ready in 1 hour and 25 minutes.

1 cup **almond flour**
1/3 cup **coconut flour**
1/3 cup **tapioca powder**
1 tbs **cinnamon** (ground)
½ cup **coconut sugar**
1 tsp **baking powder**
1 tsp **baking soda**
1 tbs **cocoa powder**
½ tsp **salt**
1 ½ tbs **raw honey**
¼ cup **coconut oil** (melted)
4 **pastured eggs** (beaten)
1 **orange** (juiced, zested)
1 ½ tsp **lemon zest** (grated)
¼ cup **pecans** (chopped)
2 cups **carrots** (grated)
5 **figs** (dried, chopped)
½ cup **raisins**
2 tbs **poppy seeds**

Makes 12 servings
Calories: 285 per serving

Preheat oven to 350°F (180°C). Lightly grease a 9 inch (23 cm) Bundt pan.
In a bowl, combine flours, coconut sugar, cinnamon, cocoa, baking powder, baking soda and salt. Mix well.

In another bowl, combine honey with oil, eggs and orange juice. Whip until blended. Add this mixture to first bowl. Mix until a batter is formed. If needed, add water to attain desired consistency. Add the rest of the ingredients and mix until well incorporated. Add more water, if needed.

Bake for about 70 minutes, or until a toothpick comes out clean if inserted at the center. Remove and let cool on wire rack. Slice into 12 wedges and serve.

Enjoy!

5. Apple Cinnamon Cake

Surprisingly soft and delicious bread, baked using almond flour and arrowroot powder. It is ready in 25 minutes.

2 cups **almond meal**
1 tsp **cinnamon**
½ cup **raw honey**
1 **apple** (peeled, diced)
½ tsp **baking soda**
¼ cup **arrowroot powder**
¼ cup **coconut oil** (melted)
1 pastured **egg**
1 tbs **vanilla extract**
½ tsp **sea salt**

Makes 12 servings
Calories: 215 per serving

Preheat oven to 350°F (180 ºC).

In a bowl, combine dry ingredients. Mix well and set aside. In another bowl, mix the wet ingredients until well blended. Gradually pour mixture into the flour mixture, while mixing until a batter is formed.

Transfer the batter into the greased loaf pan and bake for about 30 minutes. Remove and allow to cool on a wire rack.

Enjoy!

6. Honey Cake with Raisins

A sweet cake with raisins and honey.

2 ½ cups **almond flour**
½ tsp **Celtic sea salt**
1 tsp **baking soda**
1 tbs **cinnamon**
1½ cup **raw honey**
¼ tsp **cloves**
½ cup organic **vegetable shortening**
4 **pastured eggs**
½ cup **raisins**

Makes 8 servings
Calories: 322 per serving.

Preheat oven to 350 °F (180 °C). Lightly oil and flour-dust an 8-inch (20 cm) cake pan.

In a large bowl, combine almond flour, cinnamon, salt, baking soda, and cloves. Mix well to blend.

In a separate bowl, mix eggs, honey, and shortening until smooth. Add this mixture to the first bowl and mix until batter is formed. Fold in raisins.

Transfer the batter to the cake pan and bake for about 30 minutes, or until toothpick comes out clean when inserted at the center. Remove from the oven and let cool on a wire rack.

Section 3: Pie recipes

1. Paleo Cheese Sauce Replacement

This is a paleo replacement for cheese sauce, which is needed for recipes 3 and 4 in this section, but can be used for all kinds of recipes.

½ cup **coconut butter** (softened)
3 tbs **coconut milk**
1 ½ tbs **lemon juice**
2 tbs **nutritional yeast**
½ clove **garlic** (crushed)
5 tbs **carrot** (finely grated)
½ cup **coconut oil** (melted)
½ tsp **sea salt**

Makes 1 cup
Calories: 154 per cup

In a heavy duty blender, combine the first 6 ingredients. Blend until smooth.

Gradually add the carrots and coconut oil while blending. Pour the mixture into a shallow container and refrigerate until needed.

Enjoy!

2. Lime Pie

A tasty lime pie with an almond-dates crust and tangy coconut milk filling. It is done in about 1 hour.

Crust:
4 pitted **dates**
1 ½ cups whole **almonds**
1 tbs **coconut oil**

Filling:
2 tbs **coconut flour**
1 cup **coconut milk**
½ cup **lime juice**
4 tsp **lime zest**
3 tbs **raw honey**
3 pastured **eggs** (beaten)

Makes 8 servings
Calories: 345 per serving

Preheat oven to 350°F (180°C). Grease a 9 inch (23 cm) pie pan.

In a food processor, combine almonds, dates, and coconut oil. Process until just short of having a nut-butter consistency.

Spread mixture in the bottom and sides of the prepared pie pan. Bake for about 7 minutes or until light brown.

Meanwhile, prepare filling. In a bowl, combine all filling ingredients and mix with a hand mixer, until well blended. Evenly spread into freshly baked pie crust and bake for another 25-30 minutes, or until well set. Remove and let cool on a wire rack.

3. Chicken Pot Pie

A chicken pot pie made with coconut and tapioca flours, using the paleo cheese from recipe 2a on the previous page. It is ready in 45 minutes.

2 cups **chicken** (cooked)
1 tbs **olive oil**
3 celery **ribs** (diced)
2 **leeks** (chopped)
½ **shallot** (minced)
½ cup **chicken stock**
¼ cup **coconut milk**
1 tbs **tapioca flour**
1/3 cup **tapioca flour**
1/3 cup **coconut flour**
2 tsp **baking soda**
2 **green onions** (chopped)
8 oz. (225 g) dairy-free **cheese** (shredded)
½ cup **water**
Paleo Cheese Sauce Replacement (recipe 1)
Sea salt

Makes 6 servings
Calories: 210 per serving

Make the paleo cheese sauce replacement from recipe 1, if you have not done so already.

Preheat oven to 350°F (180°C).

In a large saucepan, heat olive oil over medium-high heat. Cook celery, leeks and shallot until tender. Mix in chicken stock, coconut milk, tapioca flour, and chicken. Reduce heat to medium and continue until cooked through. Season with salt to taste.

In a bowl, combine flours, green onions, baking soda, and the paleo cheese sauce replacement. Gradually add tablespoons of water while mixing until crumbly.

Evenly spread vegetable mix into a baking dish. Cover everything with the crumbly mixture and bake for about 30 minutes, or until golden brown.

Enjoy!

4. Paleo Quiche

This a paleo version of a traditional French pastry. It is ready in just over 1 hour.

Crust:
1 ½ cups whole **almonds**
1 tbs **coconut oil**

Filling:
1 tsp **olive oil**
1 cup **onion** (thinly sliced)
4 **bacon** slices (browned, crumbled)
¾ cup **Cheese Sauce Replacement** (from recipe 1)
3 large pastured **eggs** (beaten)
3 large pastured **egg** whites (beaten)
1 ½ cups **almond milk**
¼ tsp **ground nutmeg**
½ tsp **salt**
¼ tsp **black pepper** (ground)

Makes 6 servings
Calories: 275 per serving

Make the paleo cheese sauce replacement from recipe 1, if you have not done so already.

Preheat oven to 350°F (180°C).

Make the crust. Process almonds and oil in a food processor until just pureed. Rub a 9 inch (23 cm) pie pan with some coconut oil. Evenly spread and press mixture on the inside of the pan. Bake for about 8 minutes or until just browned.

In a pan, heat oil over medium-high heat. Add onions and sauté for about 8 minutes. Transfer to a bowl and let cool. Evenly distribute onions, bacon, and cheese sauce replacement into the crust. Set aside.

In a bowl, whisk eggs and egg white until smooth. Mix in milk and the remaining ingredients until blended. Pour into the crust, covering the onion mixture.

Bake for about 50 minutes. Loosely cover with tin foil at half time to avoid over browning. Remove and let cool on a wire rack.

Enjoy!

5. Apple Pie

This Paleo version of classic apple pie consists of almond crust and apple filling. It is ready in about 1 hour.

Crust:
2 cups **almond flour**
¼ tbs **sea salt**
2 tbs **coconut oil**
1 **pastured egg**

Filling:
2 ½ lbs. (1.13 kg) **apples** (peeled, cut into slices)
½ cup + 2 tbs **coconut sugar**
3 tbs **almond flour**
1 tbs **vanilla extract**
1 tbs **lemon juice**
1 tsp **cinnamon**
1 large **pastured egg white**
2 tbs **fruit jam** (any)

Makes 6 servings
Calories: 273 per serving

Making the crust: In a food processor, combine almond flour and salt. While mixing, slowly add oil and egg, until a batter is formed. Spread batter on the bottom and sides of a 9 inch (23 cm) pie pan. Chill until firm.

Preheat oven to 375°F (190°C).

In a bowl, combine flour with apple slices, ½ cup coconut sugar, cinnamon, and vanilla extract. Toss to coat.

Place the coated apple slices into the crust in a concentric circle pattern. Brush edges with egg white and sprinkle coconut sugar. Bake for about 45 minutes, or until golden brown. Remove and let cool on a wire rack.

Glaze filling with any fruit jam. Slice and serve.

Enjoy!

6. Peach Pie

This peach pie features an almond-coconut crust, yogurt filling, and a peach topping. It is ready in about 3 hours.

Crust:
2 tbs **coconut butter** (melted)
1 ¼ cups **almond meal**
1 large **pastured egg white** (lightly beaten)
1 tbs **olive oil**

Filling:
2 tsp unflavored **gelatin**
1/3 cup **coconut sugar**
1/8 tsp **sea salt**
1 cup **almond milk (**divided)
1 ½ cups **coconut milk yogurt**

Topping:
1 ½ lbs. (680 g) **peaches** (cut into wedges)
2 tbs **water**
2 tsp **lemon juice**
1 tsp **coconut butter** (diced)
2 tbs **coconut sugar**

Makes 12 servings
Calories: 193 per serving

Start with the filling 2 hours before doing the rest.

In a pan, mix gelatin with ½ cup almond milk and let it stand for 3 minutes. Dissolve gelatin over medium heat. Transfer melted gelatin to a bowl and add the rest of the filling ingredients. Mix well to blend. Pour mixture into cooled crust and chill for no less than 2 hours.

Preheat oven to 350°F (180°C).

Make the crust: Process all ingredients in a food processor until well blended. Spread and press mixture into bottom and sides of a 9 inch (23 cm) pie pan and bake for about 30 minutes, or until golden brown.

Increase the oven temperature to 425°F (220°C).

Make the topping: Scatter peaches in a baking dish. Drizzle lemon juice and water, shower with coconut sugar and top with coconut butter. Bake for about 18 minutes. Remove and let it cool completely.

Arrange roasted peaches on top of the chilled pie. Slice and serve.

Enjoy!

Section 4: Cupcake recipes

1. Jelly Donut Cupcakes

These cupcakes make use of fruit jam, which means their flavor is easy to vary. They are ready in about 40 minutes.

½ cup **coconut** oil (melted)
½ cup **applesauce**
3 tbs **raw honey**
1 tbs **vanilla extract**
3 **pastured eggs**
½ cup **coconut flour**
1 tbs **almond milk**
¼ tsp **baking soda**
½ cup **fruit jam** (any)
½ tsp **sea salt**

Makes 12 cupcakes
Calories: 178 per cup cake

Preheat oven to 350°F (180°C). Prepare parchment paper-lined 12 muffin cups.

In a food processor, combine coconut oil, applesauce, eggs, vanilla extract and raw honey. Process until well blended. Transfer to a bowl, gradually add flour, baking soda and salt. Mix until a batter is formed. If needed, add more almond milk to attain desired consistency.

Spoon batter into muffin cups until they are ¾ full. Add spoonful portions of any fruit jam (apricot, raspberry etc.) to each cup and swirl to mix slightly. Bake for about 25 minutes, or until toothpick comes out clean if inserted at the center.

2. Paleo Chocolate Cupcakes

This is a chocolate dessert made with coconut flour, coconut oil and pastured eggs. It uses a glazing made in recipe 5 of section 1.

½ cup **coconut flour**
¼ cup **cocoa powder**
¼ tsp **sea salt**
½ tsp **baking soda**
3 large **pastured eggs**
4 tbs **coconut oil**
½ cup **honey**
Hot chocolate (from recipe 5, section 1, optional)

Makes 10 servings
Calories: 69 per serving

If you wish to use the hot chocolate glazing, prepare it according to recipe 5 of section 1.

Preheat oven to 350°F (180°C). Prepare a 12 cup muffin pan lined with paper liners.

In a bowl, combine all dry ingredients and mix well. In separate bowl, whisk eggs, oil, and honey until smooth.

Slowly add the dry mixture while mixing, until a batter is formed. Fill muffin cups with batter and bake for about 20 minutes. Remove from the oven and let cool on a wire rack.

Optionally, top cupcakes with the hot chocolate.

Enjoy!

3. Ginger Cupcakes with Paleo Cream

This is a paleo version of classic ginger cupcakes. They are ready in about 30 minutes.

1 cup + 3 tbs **almond flour**
1/3 cup **coconut flour**
1 tsp **ginger** (ground)
¼ tsp **nutmeg** (freshly grated)
¼ tsp **sea salt**
⅛ tsp **baking powder**
¼ tsp **baking soda**
6 tbs **coconut butter**
½ tsp **vanilla extract**
2/3 cup **raw honey**
4 tsp **lemon zest** (finely grated)
1 **pastured egg**
1-inch (2.5 cm) **ginger** (finely grated)
½ cup **paleo cream** (see below)
¼ cup **ginger** (finely chopped)

Paleo Cream:
1 cup **coconut milk** (chilled)
2 tbs **lemon juice** or **apple cider vinegar**
⅛ tsp **sea salt**

Makes 36 mini cupcakes
Calories: 47 per cupcake

Make the paleo cream: Combine cream, lemon juice and salt. Whisk to blend. Adjust to desired taste.

Preheat oven to 350°F (180°C). Line three 12 cup muffin pans with paper liners.

In a bowl, combine flours with nutmeg, ginger, salt, baking soda, and baking powder. Mix well and set aside.

In a bowl, beat butter using a hand mixer until smooth. Add 3 tbs raw honey, vanilla extract, lemon zest and ginger. Beat for about 1 minute. Gradually add more honey and beat after each addition. Add the egg and beat for 1 more minute until very smooth.

Slowly add the flour mixture, paleo cream, and ginger. Mix until well blended.

Transfer mixture to prepared muffin pans until they are ¾ full. Bake for about 18 minutes, or until light brown and fluffy. Remove from the oven and let cool on a wire rack. Remove cupcakes and let cool off completely.

Enjoy!

4. Almond-Banana Cupcakes

These cupcakes are colored with natural beet juice and frosted with dairy-free yogurt. They are ready in 35 minutes.

Cupcakes:
1 cup **almond flour**
¼ cup **coconut flour**
¾ cup **coconut sugar**
1/3 cup **cocoa powder**
1 tsp **baking soda**
2 **pastured eggs** (beaten)
1 tbs **vanilla** extract
½ tsp **beet juice**
1/3 cup **banana** (mashed)
1 cup **almond milk**
1 tsp **apple cider vinegar**
½ tsp **sea salt**

Frosting:
1 cup **almond milk yogurt**
3 tbs **raw honey**
½ tsp **vanilla extract**

Makes 12 cupcakes
Calories: 67 per serving

Preheat oven to 350°F (180°C). Prepare 12 cup muffin pan lined with paper liners.

In a large bowl, combine flours along with all other dry cupcake ingredients. Set aside.

In another bowl, beat the eggs. Add the remaining ingredients. Mix well to blend, then transfer to the flour mixture. Mix until well incorporated and a batter is formed.

Fill muffin cups with the batter and bake for 20-25 minutes, or until a toothpick comes out clean when inserted at the center of a cupcake. Remove and let cool on a wire rack.

In a bowl, whisk all frosting ingredients together until smooth. Spread on top of each cupcake.

Enjoy!

5. Vanilla Cupcakes

These vanilla cupcakes are ready in 45 minutes.

1 ¼ cups **almond flour**
½ cup **coconut flour**
1 ½ tsp **baking powder**
½ tsp **sea salt**
3 tbs **coconut butter** (softened)
1 cup **raw honey**
3 tbs **coconut oil**
4 **pastured eggs**
½ cup **applesauce**
½ cup **almond milk**
½ tsp **vanilla extract**

Makes 12 cupcakes
Calories: 76 per serving

Preheat oven to 350°F (180°C). Prepare 12 cup muffin pans lined with paper liners.

In a bowl, mix flours, baking powder, and salt. Set aside.

Using a hand mixer, beat butter in a bowl for about 3 minutes until smooth. Slowly add ½ of the honey and beat for about 2 minutes. Add oil and remaining honey, beat for another 2 minutes or until light and smooth. One by one, add eggs and beat after each addition. Add applesauce and beat until well blended.

Add the flour mixture, almond milk, and vanilla extract, then beat until fully incorporated.

Fill cups with the batter and bake for about 23 minutes, or until a toothpick comes out clean if inserted at the center of a cupcake. Remove from the oven and let cool completely.

Section 5: Cookie recipes

1. Fruity Almond Cookies

These are very light cookies with applesauce, cranberries and pecans. They are ready in 25 minutes.

3 cups **almond flour**
1 tbs **coconut oil**
2 cups **applesauce**
1 ½ tsp **baking soda**
½ cup **coconut sugar**
½ cup **pecans** (chopped)
½ cup **cranberries** (dried)
2 **pastured eggs** (beaten)
¼ cup **coconut flour**
2 tsp **cinnamon** (ground)

Makes 24 cookies
Calories: 113 per serving

Preheat oven to 400°F (200°C). Prepare 2 baking sheets lined with paper liners and lightly brushed with coconut oil.

In a bowl, dissolve baking soda in applesauce. Gradually add the rest of the ingredients. Mix after adding each ingredient and continue until a smooth batter is formed.

Drop spoonful portions on the prepared baking sheet, lightly press each cookie and bake for about 15 minutes. Remove and let cool on a wire rack.

Enjoy!

2. Pumpkin Cookies

These pumpkin cookies are perfect for Halloween and Thanksgiving. They are prepared and baked in about 40 minutes.

2 cups **almond meal**
½ tsp **baking soda**
½ cup **coconut oil** (melted)
½ cup **pumpkin puree**
1 tbs **pumpkin pie spice**
½ tsp **sea salt**
¼ cup unsweetened **coconut** (shredded)
1 tbs pure **vanilla extract**
½ cup **raw honey**

Makes 15 servings
Calories: 85 per serving

Preheat oven to 350°F (180°C). Line a baking sheet with parchment paper.

In a bowl, combine all ingredients and blend using a hand mixer until a batter has formed. Drop 1-tbs-portions of batter onto prepared baking sheet and bake for about 30 minutes. Remove and let cool on a wire rack.

Enjoy!

3. Macadamia Chocolate Cookies

In this recipe, macadamia is turned into nut butter and baked with coconut flour and chocolate chips. These cookies take about 40 minutes to make.

2 tbs **coconut flour**
1 cup **macadamia nut butter**
¼ cup **coconut oil**
1 tsp **vanilla extract**
¼ cup **raw honey**
1 **pastured egg**
½ cup **dark chocolate chips**
1 pinch of **sea salt**

Macadamia nut butter
6 tbs **coconut oil**
1 lb. **macadamia nuts**
1 pinch **sea salt**
5 tbs raw **honey** (optional)

Makes 8 servings
Calories: 97 per serving

Preheat oven to 350°F (180°C). Line 2 baking sheets with parchment paper.

In a food processor, combine all ingredients for the macadamia nut butter and process to desired consistency.

In a bowl, combine nut butter with coconut oil, honey, vanilla and egg. Blend with a hand mixer until a smooth batter has formed. Fold in chocolate chips. Chill for about 15 minutes.

Drop 2-tbs-portions of batter on prepared baking sheets and bake for 15 minutes. Remove and let cool on a wire rack. Serve warm.

4. Honey Coconut Macaroons

This recipe contains only 4 ingredients, but represents a great treat for coconut lovers. It is ready in about 40 minutes.

2 large **egg whites**
¼ cup **raw honey**
¼ tsp **sea salt**
2 ½ cups **coconut flakes**

Makes 8 servings
Calories: 86 per serving

Preheat oven to 350°F (180°C). Line a baking sheet with parchment paper.

In a bowl, whisk egg whites with honey and salt until smooth. Add coconut flakes, mix until incorporated. Refrigerate for about 30 minutes.

Drop 2-tbs-portions of batter onto prepared baking sheet and bake for about 10 minutes, or until golden brown. Remove and let cool on a wire rack.

Enjoy!

5. Chocolate Carrot Cookies

These cookies can be prepared and baked in 40 minutes.

1 cup **coconut flour**
½ cup **tapioca flour**
2 large **carrots** (shredded)
1 cup **coconut sugar**
1 cup **coconut oil** (melted)
2 **pastured eggs** (beaten)
1 tsp **vanilla**
½ tsp **pumpkin pie spice**
Sea salt (to taste)
½ cup **chocolate chips**
    or self-made **paleo chocolate**

Makes 12 servings
Calories: 186 per serving

Preheat oven to 350°F (180°C). Line a cookie sheet with parchment paper.

Whisk eggs in a bowl, then add oil, coconut sugar and vanilla extract. Mix to blend.
Add carrots, flours and spices. Mix well. Fold in chocolate chips or the self-made paleo chocolate from recipe 1, section 1.

Spoon batter onto prepared baking sheet, press to flatten and bake for about 30 minutes. Remove and let cool on a wire rack.

Enjoy!

Section 6: Frozen Desserts

1. Banana Pecan Ice Cream

This quick treat is ready in just 5 minutes.

2 **bananas** (chopped, frozen)
1 tbs **raw honey**
1 tsp **vanilla extract**
1 pinch **sea salt**
½ cup **pecans**

Makes 2 servings
Calories: 142 per serving

Partially thaw bananas. Transfer to a food processor along with honey, vanilla and salt. Process to puree. Add pecans and pulse to desired nut sizes. Serve immediately.

Enjoy!

2. Paleo Banana-Chocolate Ice Cream

This ice cream recipe is a real treat and uses the paleo mousse chocolate of recipe 6 in section 1.

2 ripe **bananas** (chopped, frozen)
1/3 cup **paleo mousse chocolate**
Cocoa nibs (for garnish)

Makes 2 servings
Calories: 143 per serving

Make the paleo mousse chocolate as described in recipe 6 of section 1. The mousse needs to be cool, so it should be refrigerated before you go on.

Slightly thaw frozen bananas. Transfer to a food processor along with the mousse chocolate. Process until desired ice cream consistency is attained.

Garnish with cocoa nibs and serve immediately.

Enjoy!

3. Strawberry Sorbet

A quick and easy sorbet that is ready in 25 minutes. It can be varied by using other types of berries.

2 cups **strawberries** (cut tops)
¼ cup **almond milk**
Mint

Makes 4 servings
Calories: 72 per serving

Puree strawberries in a food processor. Add almond milk and some mint, then process until the mixture is well blended.

Transfer to the freezer and wait for about 20 minutes, or until desired thickness is attained. Serve and enjoy!

Enjoy!

4. Creamy Berry Smoothie

This smoothie is perfect on hot days. It is made with almond milk yogurt and takes 2 minutes to be ready.

2 cups **orange juice**
1 cup **almond milk yogurt**
2 small **ripe bananas**
¼ tsp **vanilla**
1 cup **any berries** (fresh or frozen)

Makes 4 servings
Calories: 91 per serving

Simply blend all ingredients in a food processor until smooth.

Enjoy!

5. Pumpkin Ice Cream

A pumpkin ice cream with creamy coconut milk. Like all pumpkin recipes, this is perfect for Halloween or Thanksgiving.

1 cup **coconut milk**
¼ cup **raw honey**
½ tbs **pumpkin pie spice**
½ cup **pumpkin (pureed)**
1 tsp **vanilla extract**
½ cup **pecans**
Cinnamon (ground)

Makes 4 servings
Calories: 172 per serving

Combine all ingredients in a food processor and process until desired chunkiness of pecans is reached.

Transfer the mixture to an ice cream machine and use it according to its instructions.

Sprinkle with cinnamon.

Enjoy!

Section 7: Muffin and Waffle Recipes

1. Pumpkin Muffins

Delicious pumpkin muffins that are ready in 35 minutes.

1 ½ cups **almond flour**
1 tsp **baking powder**
1 tsp **baking soda**
½ tsp **cinnamon** (ground)
1 ½ tsp **pumpkin pie spice**
1/8 tsp **sea salt**
¾ cup **canned pumpkin**
3 large **eggs**
¼ cup **raw honey**
2 tsp **almond butter**
2 tbs **almonds** (slivered)

Makes 6 servings
Calories: 97 per serving

Preheat oven to 350°F (180°C). Lightly grease muffin cups.

In a bowl, combine flour with the next 6 ingredients.

In a separate bowl, beat eggs, honey and almond butter until smooth. Transfer to the flour mixture. Mix until batter is formed.

Bake for about 25 minutes on the middle rack, or until golden brown. Remove from the oven and sprinkle almonds on top. Let muffins cool before serving.

2. Omelet Bacon Waffles

This recipe sandwiches omelet and bacon in between waffles, which is perfect for breakfast. It is done in 12 minutes.

Waffle:
1 cup **almond flour**
½ cup **tapioca flour**
2 tbs **coconut flour**
1 tsp **baking soda**
½ tsp **sea salt**
4 **pastured eggs**
1/3 cup **coconut milk**
2 tbs **coconut oil**
2 tsp **vanilla extract**

Topping
2 slices **bacon**
2 tsp **olive oil** (divided)
2 **pastured eggs**
2 tbs **chives** (chopped)
¼ tsp **pepper**
¼ cup **raw honey**

Makes 4 servings
Calories: 174 per serving

In a large bowl, combine all dry waffle ingredients. Mix well and set aside.

In another bowl, beat eggs, then add the rest of the wet waffle ingredients and mix until well blended. Slowly pour flour mixture into the wet mixture, Mix until a batter has formed. Let it stand for about 5 minutes.

Transfer batter to the waffle maker and use it according to the instruction manual.

Preheat oven to 400°F (200°C).

In a saucepan, heat oil over medium-high heat. Add bacon and brown for about 3 minutes. Drain on paper towel-lined plate.

For the topping: In a bowl, beat eggs, then add chives and pepper. Mix to blend. Add more oil to the saucepan and stir-fry egg mixture over medium-low flame for about 5 minutes, or until well cooked.

Place 4 waffles on a baking sheet. Layer ¼ of the scrambled eggs, bacon, and dairy-free cheese on each of the waffles. Top each waffle with the remaining 4 waffles.

Transfer to the oven and bake for about 4 minutes, or until crisp.

Drizzle honey and serve immediately.

Enjoy!

3. Paleo Spinach Muffins

These egg muffins are made with almond milk and dairy-free cheese. They are ready in 35 minutes.

8 large **eggs**
½ cup **almond milk**
1 cup **dairy-free cheese** (shredded)
1 cup **spinach** (shredded)
Sea salt and ground **black pepper**
1 tbs **coconut butter**
Fresh basil (minced)

Makes 4 servings
Calories: 214 per serving

Preheat oven to 350°F (180°C). Lightly grease a 12-cup muffin pan.

In a bowl, beat eggs and milk. Add the rest of the ingredients and season with salt and pepper. Mix until a batter has formed.

Fill muffin cups with batter and bake for about 30 minutes, or until golden brown. Remove and let cool on a wire rack.

Enjoy!

4. Coconut-Banana-Strawberry Waffles

These coconut-banana-strawberry waffles are perfect on a cold winter evening.

½ cup **coconut flour**
¼ tsp **baking soda**
¼ cup **coconut milk**
8 **pastured eggs**
½ cup **coconut butter**
¼ tsp **sea salt**

Topping
2 sliced **strawberries**
1 tbs **almond butter**
½ **small banana**
2 tsp **raw honey**

Makes 4 servings
Calories: 102 per serving

Preheat a waffle maker.

In a food processor, combine all ingredients. Process until a batter has formed. Transfer batter to the waffle maker and use it according to the instruction manual.

Serve topped with almond butter, mashed strawberries and banana slices. Drizzle raw honey on top.

Enjoy!

5. Banana-Cinnamon Waffles

Another waffle recipe that is perfect for cold winter evenings.

2 tsp **cinnamon** (ground)
1 tsp **sea salt**
4 **pastured eggs**
¼ cup **almond flour**
½ cup **coconut flour**
½ cup **tapioca flour**
1 large **banana**
1 cup **coconut milk**
1/3 cup **coconut oil** (melted)
2 tsp. **vanilla extract**
2 tbs **raw honey**

Makes 4 servings
Calories: 125 per serving

Preheat a waffle maker.

In a food processor, combine all ingredients. Process until a batter has formed.

Transfer batter to the waffle maker and use it according to the instruction manual.

Enjoy!

Section 8: Bread and Buns

1. Flaxseed Bread

This delicious bread is made with a combination of coconut and almond flours. It goes very well with homemade fruit jam.

2 tbs **coconut flour**
1 ½ cups **almond flour**
¼ cup **golden flaxseed**
1 ½ tsp **baking soda**
¼ cup **coconut oil**
1 tbs **raw honey**
5 **pastured eggs**
1 tbs **apple cider vinegar**
¼ tsp **sea salt**

Makes 8 servings
Calories: 243 per serving

Preheat the oven to 350°F (180°C). Lightly grease a loaf pan with coconut oil.

In a food processor, combine all dry ingredients. Pulse to blend. Gradually add in wet ingredients while pulsing until a batter is formed.

Evenly spread batter into the prepared loaf pan and bake for about 30 minutes. Remove and let cool on a wire rack.

Enjoy!

2. Pumpkin-Blueberry Bread

A pumpkin bread that is perfect for Halloween and Thanksgiving.
It is ready in about 1 hour.

½ cup **macadamia nuts**
1 cup **cashew nuts**
Macadamia nut oil
1 cup **pumpkin puree**
1 cup **almond meal**
1 ripe **banana** (chopped)
1 tsp **baking powder**
2 **pastured eggs**
1 tsp **baking soda**
2 tsp **cinnamon**
½ tsp **pumpkin pie spice**
Coconut oil (for greasing)
1 cup **blueberries**
1 pinch **sea salt**

Makes 12 slices
Calories: 92 per slice

Preheat oven to 375°F (190 °C).

In a food processor, combine cashews and macadamia nuts.
Process into a fine nut meal.

Add macadamia nut oil while processing until a smooth butter is
attained. Add in bananas and pumpkin puree and mix until a thick
batter is formed.

In a large bowl, beat eggs. Add banana-nut mixture and the rest of
the ingredients except for the berries. Mix well until fully
incorporated. Fold in the berries.

Lightly oil a bread pan and evenly spread batter into it. Transfer to the oven and bake for about 50 minutes, or until toothpick comes out clean when inserted at the center. Remove and let cool for 10 minutes before serving.

Enjoy!

3. Banana Bread

A delicious banana bread with chocolate and cinnamon. It is ready in about 1 hour.

Chocolate swirl:
1 cup **dark chocolate** (cut into chunks)
1 tsp **coconut oil**
1 tbs **coconut butter**
2 tbs **cinnamon**

Banana bread:
4 ripe medium **bananas**
½ cup **coconut flour**
1 tsp **baking soda**
½ cup **almond butter**
4 large **pastured eggs**
Coconut oil (for greasing)
1/8 tsp **sea salt**

Makes 6 servings
Calories: 295 per serving

For the chocolate swirl: Place chocolate chunks, butter and coconut oil in a bowl. Place the bowl over a pot with simmering water to melt the ingredients. Mix to blend. Add cinnamon and mix again. Set aside.

For the banana bread: Preheat the oven to 350°F (180°C). Lightly grease a loaf pan with coconut oil.

In a large bowl, mash bananas, then add flour, baking powder and salt. Mix to blend.

In a separate bowl, beat eggs with almond butter until creamy. Pour into the banana mixture and mix well.

Transfer ½ of this mixture to the prepared pan, add 2 tbs of melted chocolate mixture and swirl with a fork. Pour the remaining banana mixture and add another chocolate mix. Swirl to form patterns.

Bake for about 50 minutes, or until knife comes out clear when inserted at the center. Remove and let cool before serving.

Enjoy!

4. Fluffy White Bread

This white bread is ready in just over 2 hours.

¼ cup **coconut flour**
½ cup **tapioca flour**
1 cup **arrowroot powder**
2 tbs **coconut sugar**
1 ¾ cup **almond flour**
2 ½ tsp **dry yeast**
1 tbs **flaxseeds** (ground)
3 **pastured eggs**
¼ cup + 1 ½ tsp **olive oil**
1 ½ cups **water** (warm)
1 ½ tsp **sea salt**

Makes 8 servings
Calories: 241 per serving

In a bowl, combine all dry ingredients. Mix well and set aside.

In another bowl, whisk eggs with ¼ cup of the oil and water. Pour into the previous bowl and mix until a soft batter is formed. Add more water if needed to attain desired consistency. Set aside for 1 hour.

Preheat the oven to 350°F (180°C). Lightly grease a loaf pan with oil.

Evenly spread batter into the prepared pan and bake for about 55 minutes. Loosely cover with tin foil after 10 minutes to avoid excessive browning. Remove and let cool on wire rack.

Enjoy!

5. Fruity Muesli Bread

This fruity and nutty bread is ready in just over 1 hour.

4 **pastured eggs**
¾ cup **almond butter**
1 tbs **raw honey**
1 tsp **ground flax meal**
¼ cup **arrowroot flour**
¼ cup **almond flour**
¼ cup **apricots** (dried, chopped)
½ cup **pistachios** (chopped)
¼ cup **hazelnuts** (chopped)
½ tsp **baking soda**
1½ cup **cranberries** (dried)
¼ cup **sesame seeds**
¼ cup **sunflower seeds**
1 tsp **sea salt**

Makes 6 servings (about 12 slices)
Calories: 152 per serving

Preheat the oven to 350°F (180°C). Grease a loaf pan and lightly coat with almond flour.

In a bowl, combine almond butter, honey, and eggs. Whisk until smooth. Set aside.

In another bowl, combine flours, meals, baking soda and salt. Mix well. Gradually pour into the wet mixture and mix until fully incorporated. Fold in nuts, seeds and fruits.

Evenly spread batter into the prepared pan and bake for about 1 hour, or until toothpick comes out clean when inserted at the center. Remove and let cool on a wire rack.

Section 9: Bagels, Pretzels, Tortillas

1. Coconut Bagels with Seeds

These delicious seed bagels take about 25 minutes to make.

¼ cup **sunflower seeds**
¼ cup **pumpkin seeds**
1 tbs **arrowroot powder**
½ tsp **unrefined sea salt**
2 tbs **coconut flour**
1 tbs **hemp seeds**
2 tsp **poppy seeds**
½ tsp **cream of tartar**
¼ tsp **baking soda**
4 **pastured eggs**
3 tbs **coconut oil**

Makes 6 bagels
Calories: 98 per bagel

Preheat the oven to 350°F (180°C). Grease a donut pan with coconut oil.

In a food processor, combine sunflower and pumpkin seeds and process to coarse bits. Add the rest of the dry ingredients and pulse several times to combine.

In a large bowl, whisk eggs with coconut oil. Add the contents of the food processor and mix until a batter has formed. Set aside for a couple of minutes. Add more water if needed to attain desired consistency.

Fill donut cups with batter and bake for about 15 minutes, or until edges start to brown. Remove and let cool on a wire rack.

2. Pumpkin Bagels

These pumpkin bagels take about 35 minutes to make.

1/3 cup **coconut flour**
3 tbs **golden flax meal**
½ tsp **cinnamon**
1 ¼ tsp **pumpkin pie spice**
3 **pastured eggs** (beaten)
2 tbs **coconut oil** (melted)
¼ cup **almond milk**
½ cup **pumpkin puree**
1 tsp **vanilla extract**
1½ tbs **raw honey**
½ tsp **baking soda**
1 tsp **apple cider vinegar**
⅛ tsp **sea salt**

Makes 8 bagels
Calories: 92 per bagel

Preheat the oven to 350°F (180°C). Grease a donut pan with coconut oil.

In a bowl, combine all of the dry ingredients, except the baking soda. Mix well and set aside.

In a separate bowl, whisk eggs. Add the rest of the wet ingredients and baking soda. Mix to blend. Pour the wet mixture into the flour mixture and stir until a batter has formed.

Scoop batter into the prepared donut pan. Bake for about 25 minutes or until browned. Remove and let cool on a wire rack.

Enjoy!

3. Soft Pretzels

These pretzels are both delicious and crunchy. They are ready in 30 minutes.

3 cups **tapioca starch**
2 cups **coconut flour**
1 tbs active **dry yeast**
1 ½ cup **warm water**
1/3 cup **coconut sugar**
4 tbs **baking soda**
Sea salt (to taste)

Makes 6 servings
Calories: 45 per serving

Preheat oven to 475°F (250 °C).

In a bowl, dissolve yeast in warm water. Add flour and coconut sugar, then mix until a batter has formed. Roll batter to form elongated thin rolls and form the traditional pretzel forms.

Fill a saucepan with 2 cups of water. Dissolve baking soda and bring to a boil over medium-high heat.

Dip pretzels into boiling water for about 15 seconds, or until golden. Place pretzels on a salted baking sheet, sprinkle salt and bake for about 10 minutes, or until golden brown.

Enjoy!

4. Paleo Tortillas

These paleo tortillas are ready in 30 minutes.

¼ cup **coconut flour**
¾ cup **almond flour**
½ cup **tapioca flour**
½ cup **tapioca starch**
1 tsp **baking powder**
¼ cup **coconut butter**
1 cup **warm water**
1 tsp **sea salt**

Makes 10 servings
Calories: 89 per serving

In a bowl, combine all dry ingredients. Add coconut butter and mix until crumbly. Add ½ cup of warm water and mix. Gradually add more water while mixing until a smooth batter is formed.

Form 8 dough balls, cover with a moist towel and work on them one ball at a time. Roll each into a circular disc, 6 inch (15 cm) in diameter. Cook in a hot skillet for several seconds until bubbly. Flip and cook the other side.

Enjoy!

5. Spiced Paleo Tortillas

These chili tortillas take 20 minutes to make.

6 **egg whites**
4 tbs **coconut flour**
4 tbs **almond milk**
½ tsp **cumin** (ground)
½ tsp **chili powder**
¼ tsp **garlic salt**
½ tsp **sea salt**

Makes 8 servings
Calories: 35 per serving

In a bowl, combine all ingredients. Mix well and set aside for a few minutes. Add more liquid if needed to attain desired soft consistency.

Grease a non-stick skillet with coconut oil and pour batter at the center. Spread batter and make it as thin as possible by tilting the pan until having a diameter of 6 inches (15 cm).

Heat for about 1 minute, or until batter is firm. Flip and cook for about 30 seconds on the other side. Work in batches.

Enjoy!

Section 10: Pancakes and Brownies

1. Paleo Pumpkin Pancakes

Like all pumpkin recipes, these pancakes are perfect for Halloween and Thanksgiving. They are ready in 20 minutes.

½ cup **pumpkin puree**
4 **pastured eggs** (beaten)
1 tsp **vanilla extract**
2 tbs **raw honey**
1 tsp **pumpkin pie spice**
¼ tsp **baking soda**
1 tsp **cinnamon**
2 tbs **coconut oil**

Makes 2 servings
Calories: 110 per serving

In a bowl, whisk the eggs. Add vanilla, honey and pumpkin puree. Mix until smooth. Add baking soda and spices. Mix until well blended.

Grease a non-stick skillet with coconut oil and pour batter at the center. Spread batter and make it as thin as possible by tilting the pan until having a diameter of 6 inches (15 cm).

Heat for about 1 minute, or until batter is firm. Flip and cook for about 30 seconds on the other side. Work in batches.

Serve with honey and coconut oil on top.

Enjoy!

2. Almond Blueberry Pancakes

These almond flour pancakes are ready in 20 minutes.

3 large **pastured eggs**
1 tbs **vanilla extract**
2 tbs **raw honey**
1 tbs **water**
1 ½ cups **almond flour**
¼ tsp **baking soda**
1 tbs **olive oil** (plus more as needed)
¼ tsp **sea salt**
Blueberries, honey, almonds (for serving)

Makes 2 servings
Calories: 120 per serving

In a bowl, whisk egg until smooth. Add vanilla, honey and water. Mix until blended. Gradually add almond flour, baking soda, and salt. Mix to combine.

Grease a non-stick skillet with oil and pour batter at the center. Spread batter and make it as thin as possible by tilting the pan until having a diameter of 6 inches (15 cm).

Heat for about 1 minute, or until batter is firm. Flip and cook for about 30 seconds on the other side. Work in batches.

Serve with chopped almonds, blueberries, and honey.

Enjoy!

3. Carrot Scallion Pancakes

These pancakes are ready in 20 minutes.

3 **scallions** (finely chopped)
½ tsp **coconut flour**
3 cups **carrots** (shredded)
3 **pastured eggs** (whipped)
Olive oil (for frying)
½ tsp **sea salt**
Applesauce (for serving)

Makes 6 servings
Calories: 96 per serving

In a bowl, mix eggs with carrots, and scallions until well blended.
Add salt and flour. Mix until a batter is formed.

Heat oil in a skillet over medium heat. Scoop a tbs-portion of
batter into the skillet, spread and cook for about 1 minute per side,
or until browned and crisp. Work in batches.

Serve with applesauce and enjoy!

4. Choco-Banana Brownie

A Paleo dieter can even enjoy brownies, if the right ingredients are used. These chocolate goodies are ready in 35 minutes.

2 tsp **cocoa powder**
3 tbs **almond flour**
1 tsp **coconut flour**
1 tbs **mashed banana** (mashed)
1 **egg white**
1 tbs **almond milk**
1 tsp **coconut oil** (softened)
1 tsp **dark chocolate chips**

Makes 2 servings
Calories: 142 per serving

Preheat oven to 350°F (180°C). Lightly grease a small baking dish.

In a bowl, combine mashed bananas with egg white, oil and almond milk. Mix until well blended. Add the rest of the ingredients and mix until a batter is formed.

Evenly spread batter into the prepared baking dish and bake for about 25 minutes, or until toothpick comes out clean when inserted at the center.

Enjoy!

5. Zucchini Brownies

These flourless brownies combine the taste of zucchini, almond and vanilla. They are ready in 35 minutes.

2 cups **zucchini** (shredded)
1 cup **almond butter**
1 **pastured egg**
1 tsp **vanilla extract**
1 tsp **cinnamon**
½ tsp **nutmeg**
1/3 cup **raw honey**
½ tsp **allspice**
1 tsp **baking soda**

Makes 12 servings
Calories: 121 per serving

Preheat oven to 350°F (180°C). Lightly grease a square baking dish.

In a bowl, combine zucchini with the rest of the ingredients. Mix until well blended.

Spread in the prepared dish and bake for about 25 minutes, or until toothpick comes out clean when inserted at the center.

Enjoy!

23520156R00077

Printed in Great Britain
by Amazon